THE WORKS OF BONAVENTURE

CARDINAL SERAPHIC DOCTOR AND SAINT

*Translated from the Latin
by
José de Vinck
Docteur en Droit of Louvain University*

I

MYSTICAL OPUSCULA

PUBLISHER
ST. ANTHONY GUILD PRESS, PATERSON, N. J.

Copyright © 1960, by St. Anthony's Guild

Library of Congress Catalogue Card Number: 60-53110

NIHIL OBSTAT: Bede Babo, O. S. B., *Censor librorum*

IMPRIMATUR: James A. McNulty, *Bishop of Paterson*

September 2, 1960

Hope. Inspiration. Trust.

WE'RE SOCIAL! FOLLOW US FOR NEW TITLES AND DEALS:
FACEBOOK.COM/CROSSREACHPUBLICATIONS
@CROSSREACHPUB

AVAILABLE IN PAPERBACK AND EBOOK EDITIONS
PLEASE GO ONLINE FOR MORE GREAT TITLES
AVAILABLE THROUGH CROSSREACH PUBLICATIONS.
AND IF YOU ENJOYED THIS BOOK PLEASE CONSIDER LEAVING A
REVIEW ON AMAZON. THAT HELPS US OUT A LOT. THANKS.

© 2017 CROSSREACH PUBLICATIONS
ALL RIGHTS RESERVED, INCLUDING THE RIGHT TO REPRODUCE
THIS BOOK OR PORTIONS THEREOF IN ANY FORM WHATEVER.

CONTENTS

THE JOURNEY OF THE MIND TO GOD—A Summary of St. Bonaventure's Mystical Theology 8
   I—On Degrees of Ascent Toward God, & on Contemplating Him Through His Traces in the Universe. 10
   II—On Contemplating God in His Traces in the Perceptible World 13
   III—On Contemplating God through That Image of Him Which Is Distinguished by Natural Faculties . 17
   IV—On Contemplating God in That Image of Him Which Was Reformed by Gratuitous Gifts 20
   V—On Contemplating God's Oneness through His Name "Being" 22
   VI—On Contemplating God's Trinity in His Name "Goodness" 24
   VII—On Mental & Mystical Ravishment in Which Repose Is Given to the Soul That Rises Toward God in Ecstatical Love 27

THE TRIPLE WAY OR LOVE ENKINDLED—A Short Treatise on Mystical Progress 29
   I—On Meditation, through Which the Soul Is Cleansed, Enlightened, and Perfected 30
   II—On Prayer, through Which Our Misery Is Deplored, God's Mercy Implored, and Worship Rendered 33
   III—On Contemplation, through Which True Wisdom Is Attained 36

The Tree of Life 43
Lignum Vitae 43
A Meditation on the Life, Death, and Resurrection of Christ 43
   I. On the Mystery of the Origin 45
   II. On the Mystery of the Passion 50
   III. On the Mystery of the Glorification 56

THE MYSTICAL VINE TREATISE ON THE PASSION OF THE LORD—A Devout Meditation 62
   I—On the Properties of the Vine 62
   II—On the Pruning of the Vine 62
   III—On the Digging around the Vine 63
   IV—On the Tying of the Vine 65
   V—On the Likeness between Christ and the Vine, and First as Regards His Body 67
   VI—On the Second Likeness, That Is, the Leaves of the Vine: and First, in a General Way 69
   VII—On the Leaves of the Vine in a Particular Way, & on the First Word of Christ on the Cross ... 70
   VIII—On the Second Leaf of the Vine, or the Second Word of Christ on the Cross 70
   IX—On the Third Leaf of the Vine, or the Third Word of Christ on the Cross 71
   X—On the Fourth Leaf of the Vine, or the Fourth Word of Christ on the Cross 72
   XI—On the Fifth Leaf of the Vine, or the Fifth Word of Christ on the Cross 72
   XII—On the Sixth Leaf of the Vine, or the Sixth Word of Christ on the Cross 73
   XIII—On the Seventh Leaf of the Vine, or the Seventh Word of Christ on the Cross 74

XIV—On the Third Likeness: That Is, the Flowers of the Vine 74
XV—On the Red and Ardent Rose: In General 75
XVI—On the Rose of Love 76
XVII—On the Rose of the Passion 76
XVIII—On the First Shedding of the Blood of Jesus Christ 77
XIX—On the Second Shedding of Blood 77
XX—On the Third Shedding of Blood 78
XXI—On the Fourth Shedding of Blood 78
XXII—On the Fifth Shedding of Blood 78
XXIII—On the Sixth and Seventh Sheddings of Blood 79
XXIV—Exhortation to Contemplate the Passion and the Love of Christ 80

ON THE PERFECTION OF LIFE ADDRESSED TO SISTERS—An Outline of Spiritual Progress 82
I—On True Self-Knowledge 83
II—On True Humility 84
III—On Perfect Poverty 86
IV—On Silence and Quiet 89
V—On Assiduity in Prayer 90
VI—On Remembering the Passion of Christ 93
VII—On Perfect Love for God 96
VIII—On Final Perseverance 97

About CrossReach Publications 100
Bestselling Titles from Crossreach 100

PUBLISHER'S NOTE

With this volume of the "Mystical Opuscula" of St. Bonaventure, the St. Anthony Guild Press initiates a series of translations which are planned to cover systematically all the Seraphic Doctor's major works. The project has been a cherished one since the foundation of St. Anthony's Guild, more than thirty years ago.

This Doctor of the Church, in a lifetime crowded with absorbing activities—as ruler of his Order for almost twenty years, as Cardinal-Bishop, as director of the deliberations of an ecumenical council—yet became one of the Church's supreme expositors of the theology of love. From the first he was known to be a giant, and succeeding centuries saw almost innumerable editions of his works. Archbishop Paschal Robinson has pointed out that no writer from the Middle Ages onward has been more widely read and copied. Yet comparatively little of this interest is reflected in publications in the English tongue.

Of course, the Prince of Mystics (as Leo XIII called him) is not wholly unknown among us. So great is the power of his genius, so insistent his message to the heart and spirit, that these qualities have in some degree forced their way through whatever barriers exist. Translators of merit, both Franciscans and others, have brought over into English separate chosen opera; and these have conveyed enough of his greatness to establish it as a fact. But though he is an acknowledged master, he remains, by and large, to us a master still unread.

The modern publisher who would have a share in making St. Bonaventure more widely known has an admirable base from which to work: the definitive Quaracchi Edition of the "Opera Omnia," completed early in this century. By authorization of the Most Reverend Augustine Sépinski, Minister General of the Order of Friars Minor, the project of translation now being launched by the St. Anthony Guild Press will make use of that monument of Franciscan scholarship. The Press is additionally fortunate in its translator, Baron José de Vinck, Docteur en Droit of Louvain, who is both a distinguished linguist and an able writer.

The second and third volumes of the series are in advanced preparation, and will follow the "Mystical Opuscula" within a year.

Fr. John Forest Loviner, O. F. M.
Director of St. Anthony's Guild.

Paterson, New Jersey
Feast of St. Francis of Assisi, 1960

FOREWORD

No biographer could trace a picture of St. Bonaventure as true and complete as that which so vividly appears from his own expressive style. But the very abundance of his writings is an obstacle to the understanding of his personality; for where exactly, in the eight massive folio volumes of his "Opera Omnia," shall we look for a true portrait of the man and of the saint? This, then, is the excuse for attempting here a broad outline of such a portrait.

By nature, Bonaventure is richly lyrical and alive. Most of his thoughts are expressed in words so warm and rhythmic that they read like poetry, and give the impression of a man constricted by mere prose, a man who is forced to sing. In this, his style significantly differs from the highly intellectual style of Thomas Aquinas.

As a writer, Bonaventure is completely at ease, making the most of an elegant Latin enriched with Scholastic terms without being decadent. His deeply logical mind takes full advantage of the subtle inflections and elaborate constructions allowed by this language; to the extent, indeed, that his organically developed periods are often difficult to render in English.

As a philosopher, Bonaventure explicitly follows the Augustinian tradition, based on Plato's notion of innate ideas. Thus, he accepts St. Anselm's ontological argument as a proof of God's existence; he seeks God rather by intuition than by reasoning; he follows the way of mysticism much more than that of philosophy proper. In this, again, he widely differs from Aquinas.

As a theologian, Bonaventure reaches into the abyss of the Trinity with such insight as to shed brilliant light upon revelation, while emphasizing the unfathomable depth of the Mystery. The Trinity is the natural framework of his mind. Time and again, he reduces rational series to these three: Power, Truth, and Goodness—Father, Son, and Holy Spirit.

As a saint, Bonaventure burns with the love of God and with the apostolic desire to spread that love abroad. He speaks of spiritual matters with the assurance of one familiar with the highest mystical reaches, almost as if he were already living in the heavenly Jerusalem. And he does this with such vividness and warmth, such convinced faith and burning charity, that his words exert an undefinable power over the reader. We forget this is a medieval scholar, a man who lived many hundreds of years ago; instead, we listen to the living words, the words of life, of a man himself very much alive.

Great saints have not invariably been great writers. Bonaventure is one of the most brilliant exceptions. Here is a man of the highest wisdom and culture, endowed with a rare gift of expression, who combines intense apostolic charity with great literary and poetical talent. The resulting work is delightful to read in the original Latin once the primary obstacles are overcome: the difficulties of the language itself, and the structure of Scholastic thought. Too few educated men of our day have the time to indulge in medieval Latin; and although Scholastic philosophy is taught in many colleges and universities, very little attention is given there to its literary expression. That is why it has seemed good to attempt to bring over into English such important works as these.

The Seraphic Doctor St. Bonaventure is generally less well known than the Angelic Doctor St. Thomas Aquinas. For various reasons, both intrinsic and historical, the works of Bonaventure, the greatest Franciscan theologian and philosopher, have been less widely published in recent translations than those of his universally acclaimed Dominican contemporary and friend. The disproportion is particularly evident in English. The present series is undertaken in the hope of bringing closer to the modern reader the thoughts of a spiritual master in many ways unique.

Bonaventure's style, rich and lyrical as it is, reflects several characteristics of his time which may seem strange to the modern mind. He has a tendency to interpret the Scriptures in an extremely symbolical way with which later scholars, disciplined in a more literal school of interpretation, might disagree. Again, he may use some chosen phrase or passage in a particularized sense, as against the modern scholar's practice of reading "in context." Finally, he insists, with what to some may seem disturbing realism, upon the physical features of Christ's sufferings.

The first two points may be disregarded as mere poetical license. When Bonaventure wrote, such fluency of interpretation and unfettered liberty in quotation had not yet been curtailed by that necessity for a more precise use of the Scriptural texts which arose in dealing with the events that brought the medieval period to a close. The discipline of utmost accuracy developed from the directives laid down by the Council of Trent.

But Bonaventure's realism is quite another thing. It may be repellent to some, but mainly such as have made of the crucifix an inanimate symbol; such as do not care to be reminded of the actuality of the passion. For Bonaventure, the suffering of the Son of God is the most real, the most essential fact of history: His torture is ever present, and His blood still flows. The health of mind of the true saint has never been more clearly evidenced than in the fact that Bonaventure's absorption in the passion never deviates into morbidity. His hold on the full meaning of Christ's agony and death never slackens; he envisages all the violence and cruelty, not for their impact on sensibility, but always as proof of what Divine Love has elected to suffer for human salvation. There is here no emotional sensationalism, but a strong incentive toward admiring wonder and devotion. The reader who would meditate on the passion and death of Christ could find no safer or better balanced guide than the Seraphic Doctor.

Biographical Data

Bonaventure was born in the year 1221 in Bagnorea (*Balneum Regis*) near Viterbo, Italy. He entered the Franciscan Order about 1240. After completing his studies at the University of Paris, he taught theology there for twelve years. At the age of thirty-six, he was elected Minister General of the Friars Minor, and remained in that office until 1273, when Pope Gregory X made him a Cardinal. He took a leading part in the Council of Lyons, and was instrumental in bringing about the temporary reunion of the Greek Church with Rome. The

Council was still in session when he died—in 1274, at the age of fifty-three.

In the year 1588, some three centuries after his death, St. Bonaventure (he had been canonized in 1482) was declared a Doctor of the Church. The bull "Triumphantis Hierusalem" of Pope Sixtus V, by elevating him to this new dignity, solemnly confirmed his merits as one of the greatest minds of the Christian Middle Ages.

FOOTNOTES

A word of caution is in order. Since the text that follows is a translation, and not a commentary on Bonaventure's works, some passages may seem difficult to the reader not versed in Scholastic terminology. Although an effort has been made to render most terms in modern English, certain technical expressions could not be avoided. Instead of burdening the book with footnotes that would have amounted to a compendium of Scholastic thought, it seemed preferable to limit footnotes to specific problems of translation. The reader interested in the subject may, with little effort, find all the light he needs in any one of the excellent textbooks dealing with the principles of Scholasticism.

SCRIPTURAL QUOTATIONS

In quoting the Scriptures, the general procedure has been to cite the sacred texts in the Confraternity of Christian Doctrine version, for all books which have reached translation at the time of publication of this volume. They are: the New Testament, the Pentateuch, the books of Josue, Judges, and Ruth, and the Sapiential books (*Job* to *Sirach-Ecclesiasticus*). All other books are cited in the Challoner-Douay translation.

Note also that the Challoner text is used, instead of the Confraternity text, in special cases where it serves Bonaventure's meaning more completely. These special instances show an asterisk after the Scriptural references.

ACKNOWLEDGMENTS

The woodcuts reproduced in these pages are works of medieval masters. Some were originally single-sheet prints; others, illustrations of books published in Venice, Milan, Rome, Ulm, etc., or produced by such great publishers as Buyer and Mathieu Husz in Lyons, Antoine Vérard in Paris, Pynson and Wynkyn de Worde in London, between 1482 and 1517, at the height of the early xylographic art period. Not a few are themselves illustrations of early editions of the works of Bonaventure.

Much gratitude is due to Father John Forest Loviner, O. F. M., Director of St. Anthony's Guild, for having promoted this project. Many thanks are due also to Miss Mary Kolars, Literary Editor of the St. Anthony Guild Press, for her scholarly assistance in the final revision of the copy.

J. de V.

Paterson, New Jersey
Pentecost, 1960

THE JOURNEY OF THE MIND TO GOD

Itinerarium Mentis in Deum

A Summary of St. Bonaventure's Mystical Theology

INTRODUCTORY NOTE

1) Symbolism

This important work of Bonaventure develops according to an intricate pattern of symbolism. The principal difficulty derives from the fact that three different symbols are used simultaneously:

A) The Mirror:

We should bear in mind that the early mirror had nothing of the perfection of its modern counterpart, but generally consisted in a piece of imperfectly polished silver or bronze that offered but a dim reflection of the objects placed before it. St. Paul says: We see now through a mirror, in an obscure manner. We should also remember that a mirror was not a common possession, but a relative luxury, in a sense a treasure.

In chapters I to VI, God is seen alternately THROUGH the mirror, and IN the mirror. To be seen THROUGH the mirror means that the mind is led to God THROUGH its understanding of the objects investigated; to be seen IN the mirror means that the mind perceives God acting and present IN the objects investigated (as Bonaventure himself explains in I Sent., 3:1–3).

Thus the first six chapters of the "Itinerarium" are concerned with the search for God:

- I: THROUGH *His traces in the universe;*
- II: IN *His traces in the human act of perception;*
- III: THROUGH *His image in natural mental powers;*
- IV: IN *His image in the soul reformed by grace;*
- V: THROUGH *His attribute of being;*
- VI: IN *His attribute of goodness.*

B) The Seraph:

The crucified Seraph seen in the vision of St. Francis serves as a second basis for symbolism. The two wings with which the Seraph covered his feet are related to chapters I and II (traces of God in creatures, and in the human act of perception of material beings), because both of these things are in themselves inferior to man. The middle pair of wings, with which the Seraph hovered, are related to chapters III and IV (image of God in the mental powers of man, and in his soul reformed by grace), because both of these things are at the level of man himself. The highest pair of wings, with which the Seraph covered his face, are related to chapters V and VI (God seen through His attribute of Being and in His attribute of Goodness), because both of these things are above man.

C) The Cherubim:

The Cherubim who stood above the Propitiatory serve as the symbolical basis for distinction between chapters V and VI: the first represents the approach to God through His oneness, as indicated by the attribute "Pure being"; the other stands for the approach through the Persons, indicated by the attribute "Pure goodness." The logical bond between the two Cherubim and the two approaches is rather weak: there are two of each, and both pairs represent adoration. But such symbolism, however far-fetched it may seem to us, was very meaningful to the medieval mind.

2) Trinitarian division:

Clearly visible is the systematically trinitarian method of division: almost every subject is broken down by threes, and the final subdivision, or final three, is always explained as representing the power of the Father, the wisdom of the Son, and the goodness of the Holy Spirit.

PROLOGUE

As I BEGIN, I call upon the First Beginning: the Father of Lights from whom all illumination descends, from whom *every good gift and every perfect gift* derives. I call upon the Eternal Father

MYSTICAL OPOSCULA

through His Son, our Lord Jesus Christ; through the intercession of the most blessed Virgin Mary, Mother of this same God and Lord Jesus Christ; and through blessed Francis, our leader and father. Give light to the eyes of our mind, *guide our feet into the way of peace*; that peace *which surpasses all understanding*; that peace announced and given to us by our Lord Jesus Christ, and preached again by our father Francis. For he proclaimed peace at the beginning and at the end of every sermon; he offered his wish of peace in every greeting; he longed for ecstatic peace in every contemplation, as a dweller of that Jerusalem of which the Man of Peace says—he who was peaceable with them that hated peace: *Pray for the peace of Jerusalem*. For he knew that the throne of Solomon would not stand except in peace, as it is written: *And his place is in peace: and his abode in Sion.*

2. At the example of our most blessed father Francis, I, too, was seeking peace with a longing spirit—I, a sinner unworthy in all ways, who yet had become the seventh Father General of the Brothers after the passing away of this most blessed father. At a time close to the thirty-third anniversary of the blessed man's departure,[1] it came about by divine prompting that I walked up Mount Alverno, longing to find some peace of soul at that place of peace. While I was there, meditating on the different ways of the mind's ascent to God, there came to me among other thoughts the memory of the miracle which had occurred in this very place to blessed Francis himself: the vision of a six-winged Seraph in the likeness of the Crucified. In my meditation, it was at once clear to me that this vision represented not only the contemplative rapture of our father, but also the road by which this rapture is attained.

3. The six wings may rightly indicate six degrees of illumination or six steps or paths, along which the soul may reach peace through the ecstatic leaps of Christian wisdom. Now, there is no path but through that most burning love for the Crucified which so transformed Paul the apostle when he was carried up to the third heaven that he could say: *With Christ I am nailed to the cross. It is now no longer I that live, but Christ lives in me*. This love also absorbed the mind of Francis—so much so that his spirit clearly shone through his flesh: indeed, for two years before his death, he carried in his own body the holy stigmata of the passion. Thus it is that the symbolism of the six wings of the Seraph suggests six ascending steps of illumination, starting with creatures and leading all the way up to God, to whom there is no access except through the Crucified. For *he who enters not by the door into the sheepfold, but climbs up another way, is a thief and a robber*.—If anyone enter by this door, he *shall go in and out, and shall find pastures.* Therefore, John said in the Apocalypse: *Blessed are they that wash their robes in the blood of the Lamb: that they may have a right to the tree of life and may enter in by the gates into the city*; as if saying that no one may enter the heavenly Jerusalem by contemplation unless he goes in through the blood of the Lamb as through a door. Nor is one prepared in any way for divine contemplation that leads to the ecstasies of the mind unless he is, like Daniel, *a man of desires*. Such desires are aroused in us in two different ways: the first is through the outcry of prayer, which makes us *roar with anguish of heart*; the second, through the flash of intuition, by which the mind turns itself most directly and intently toward the light.

4. First, therefore, I invite the reader to cry out in prayer through Christ crucified, by whose blood we are cleansed from the filth of sin. Let us not believe that it is enough to read without unction, to speculate without devotion, to investigate without wonder, to observe without joy, to act without godly zeal, to

---

[1] That is, around October 4, 1259.

know without love, to understand without humility, to strive without divine grace, or to reflect as a mirror without divinely inspired wisdom.

To those who are favored by divine grace, to the humble and the holy, to the repentant and the devout; to those anointed with the *oil of gladness*, to the lovers of divine wisdom, to those inflamed with the desire for it, and to those who wish to dedicate themselves to the glorification, praise, and enjoyment of God, I propose the thoughts that follow. I am supposing that the mirror offered by the outside world is of little or no value, useless, if the mirror of the mind is not clear and polished. Therefore, man of God, train yourself by heeding the sharp goad of conscience before you lift up your eyes to the beams of wisdom reflected in the mirrors of the same wisdom, lest you fall into a deeper pit of darkness for having gazed upon such light.

5. It seems fitting to divide this work into seven chapters, giving each one a separate title that will facilitate the understanding of the contents. Please consider the writer's intention rather than his performance; the sense of his words instead of their lack of polish; the truth presented in preference to the style; the training of the heart more than the erudition of the mind. To this end, let us not hasten through the development of thoughts, but dwell upon them at due length.

Chapter I—On the Degrees of the Ascent Toward God, and on Contemplating Him Through His Traces in the Universe

a) Degrees of the Ascent Toward God

1. *Blessed is the man whose help is from Thee. In his heart he hath disposed to ascend by steps, in the vale of tears, in the place which he hath set.* Since beatitude is nothing other than the enjoyment of the supreme good, and this supreme good is above us, no one can attain beatitude unless he rises above himself, not in body but in heart. Yet we cannot rise above ourselves unless a superior power lifts us up. No matter how well we plan our spiritual progress, nothing comes of it unless divine assistance intervenes. And divine assistance is there for those who seek it humbly and devoutly, who sigh for it in this *vale of tears* by fervent prayer. Prayer, then, is the mother and the beginning of the ascent. Denis, in his "Mystical Theology," intending to enlighten us in regard to mystical ecstasy, names prayer as the first condition. So let us pray and say to the Lord our God: *Teach me, O Lord, Your way, that I may walk in Your truth; direct my heart that it may fear Your name.*

2. By praying in this manner, we receive light to learn the steps of the ascent to God.

In our present condition, the created universe itself is a ladder leading us toward God. Some created things are His traces; others, His image; some of them are material, others spiritual; some temporal, others everlasting: thus some are outside us, and some within.

Now, the First Principle is wholly spiritual and eternal, and is entirely above us. In order to achieve some understanding of Him, we must first follow the traces which are material, temporal, and external. This means being conducted in the way of God. Then, we must penetrate our own mind, which is an image of God, everlasting, spiritual, and internal. This means walking in the truth of God. We must, finally, pass over to the eternal, the wholly spiritual, which is above us, by looking up to the First Principle. And this means rejoicing in the knowledge of God and in the reverence due to His majesty.

3. So this is the three-day journey into the wilderness, or the three degrees of light within a single day: dusk, dawn, and noon.[2] It represents the triple existence of things, that is, existence in physical reality, in the mind, and in the Eternal Art,[3] according to what is written: *Let it be; God made it; and it was.* It also represents the presence in Christ, our Ladder, of a triple substance, bodily, rational, and divine.

---

[2] The liturgical day begins with the office of Vespers, sung at 6 p. m., or sundown.

[3] Eternal Art, in Bonaventure, is the creative wisdom of God manifested in the Word through whom, as if through an instrument of art, God created the universe. Cf. "Commentaria in Hexaemeron," I:13.

4. Corresponding to this triple movement, our mind has three principal powers of perception. One is aimed at the material world and is called ANIMAL or SENSORIAL; the other is aimed inward and acts within itself, and is called SPIRITUAL; the third one is aimed above itself, and is called SUPERNATURAL. By these triple means, we should dispose ourselves for the knowledge of God, and love Him with our whole heart, and with our whole soul, and with our whole mind. In this consists the perfect observance of the Law, as well as full Christian wisdom.

5. Any one of the processes described above may be doubled when God is seen as both *the Alpha and the Omega*, or both THROUGH A MIRROR, and IN A MIRROR, or again when each process is considered both as overlapping the other and as standing alone. Hence, the three chief processes must be multiplied by two, becoming six in number. As God created the whole world in six days and rested on the seventh, so must the smaller world be led in an orderly way through the six successive degrees of enlightenment to the repose of contemplation. As a symbol of this, there were six steps leading up to the throne of Solomon; the Seraphim seen by Isaias had six wings; after six days, God called Moses from the midst of the cloud; and after six days, as Matthew tells us, Christ led His disciples to the mountain and was transfigured before them.

6. Parallel to the six steps of the ascent to God, the powers of the soul also have six degrees through which we rise from the depths to the heights, from the external to the internal, from the temporal to the eternal. They are the following: SENSES, IMAGINATION, REASON, UNDERSTANDING, INTELLIGENCE, and, at the tip of the mind, the spark of MORAL DISCERNMENT. These powers, implanted in us by nature, were distorted by sin, and are reformed by grace. They must be cleansed by righteousness, trained by learning, and perfected by wisdom.

7. According to the original plan of nature, man was made fit for the repose of contemplation; therefore *the Lord God took the man and placed him in the garden of Eden*. But man turned away from the true light, stooping down to unstable goods; so he was himself bent down by personal sin, and his whole posterity by original sin, which infected human nature in two ways: by ignorance in the mind, and by concupiscence in the flesh. So man, blind and bent down, is sitting in darkness, where he cannot see the light of heaven unless he is assisted by grace and righteousness against concupiscence, and by knowledge and wisdom against ignorance. This can be accomplished through Jesus Christ alone, *who has become for us God-given wisdom, and justice, and sanctification, and redemption*. Since He *is the power of God and the wisdom of God*, the Incarnate Word, *full of grace and of truth*, He is the font of grace and truth. That is, He has poured forth the grace of charity; which, stemming from *a pure heart, and a good conscience, and faith unfeigned*, straightens the whole soul according to the triple level described above. Likewise, He has taught the knowledge of truth according to the existing three methods of theology: the symbolical, the proper, and the mystical; so that by symbolical theology, we may use in the right way the sensible world; by theology proper, the world of intelligible substances; and by mystical theology, we may be ecstatically carried above the intellect.

8. Thus, whoever is anxious to ascend to God must first eliminate nature-deforming sin, then train the above-described natural powers in three ways: by prayer, to receive reforming grace; by a good life, to receive purifying righteousness; by contemplation, to receive perfecting wisdom. As no one can achieve wisdom except through grace, righteousness, and knowledge, likewise no one can achieve contemplation except through penetrating meditation, a holy life, and devout prayer. Since grace is both the foundation of right will and the source of light for the penetrating reason, we must first pray, then lead holy lives, finally concentrate our vision upon the reflections of truth, and by this contemplation, rise until we reach the mountaintop where we *shall see the God of gods in Sion*.

9. Since we have to ascend the ladder of Jacob before we can descend it, let us place the first of the ascending rungs at the bottom, by setting before ourselves the whole material world as a mirror through which we can step up to God, the supreme Craftsman. Thus we shall be true Israelites, traveling through Egypt toward the land promised to the fathers; we shall be Christians, passing with Christ *out of this world to the Father*, and we shall be lovers of the Wisdom who calls to us and says: *Come to Me,*

all you that yearn for Me, and be filled with My fruits.—For from the greatness and the beauty of created things, their original Author, by analogy, is seen.

10. The supreme power, wisdom and goodness of the Creator shine forth in created things as the senses reveal these attributes to the interior faculty in a threefold way: by assisting the mind as it investigates by reason, believes by faith, and speculates by intellect. Speculation regards things in their actual existence, faith, in their habitual course, and investigation, in their potential excellence.[4]

11. By following the first method, that of speculation, man considers things in themselves, and sees in them weight, number, and measure; weight indicating the point toward which they tend, number distinguishing them from one another, and measure determining their dimensions. Thus, man also sees in them mode, species, and order,[5] as well as substance, power, and operation. From these, as from so many traces, he can rise to the understanding of the immeasurable power, wisdom, and goodness of the Creator.

12. By following the second method, that of belief, man considers this world in its origin, development, and end. *By faith, we understand that the world was fashioned by the word of God.* By faith, we believe that three phases of law succeeded each other and ran their course in perfect order: the law of nature, the law of Scripture, and the law of grace. By faith, we believe that the world shall come to an end with the final judgment. Thus are displayed, first the power, then the providence, lastly the justice of the Supreme Principle.

13. By following the third method, that of investigation through reason, man sees that some things possess existence only, others possess existence and life, others again existence, life, and reason. The first things he sees to be lower, the second to be intermediate, and the third to be higher. He also sees that some things are only material; others, partly material and partly spiritual; from which he concludes that others still are purely spiritual, being better and of higher rank than the first two groups. He sees, finally, that some things are mutable and corruptible, as are the earthly bodies; others, mutable but incorruptible, as are the heavenly bodies; from which he notes that some others are both immutable and incorruptible, as are the beings transcending space.

From these things, which are subject to perception, man rises to the consideration of divine power, wisdom, and goodness as something existent, alive, intelligent, purely spiritual, incorruptible, and immutable.

14. This reasoning may be developed in accordance with the sevenfold characteristics of creatures, which are a sevenfold testimony to the power, wisdom, and goodness of God; that is, by considering the ORIGIN, VASTNESS, MULTITUDE, BEAUTY, FULLNESS, OPERATION, and ORDER of all things.

The ORIGIN of things, according to their creation, distinction, and lavish completion, which resulted from the work of the six days, points to a might producing everything out of nothingness, a wisdom giving all things their distinct character, and a goodness generously completing them.—The VASTNESS of things, in length, width, and depth; in the quality of their energy, which extends in length, width and depth, as appears in the diffusion of light; and in the efficiency of their operations, which are immanent, continuous, and pervasive, as appears in the operation of fire, obviously points to the immensity of the might, wisdom, and goodness of the triune God who, by His power, presence, and essence exists uncircumscribed in all things.—The MULTITUDE of things, defying all human calculation, in their generic, specific, and individual diversity of substance, form or figure, and efficiency, obviously indicates and demonstrates again the immensity of the same three qualities as they exist in God.—The BEAUTY of things, in the variety of light, shape, and color displayed in the elementary substances, such as the heavenly bodies; in the mixed substances, such as the minerals, including stones and metals; and also in the complex substances, such as plants and animals,

---

[4] This inversion of the preceding order is followed through in the development.

[5] MODE (of being) refers to the creature's dependence upon the Efficient Cause ("a Deo"—by the power of God); SPECIES refers to the creature's conformity with the Exemplary Cause ("secundum Deum"—according to God); and ORDER refers to the creature's ordination toward the Final Cause ("propter Deum"—for God as an end).

clearly proclaims once more the three aforesaid perfections.—The FULLNESS of things, by which matter is pregnant with forms through the power of the seed, form is full of energy through active potency, and energy is full of effects through actual efficiency, clearly affirms the same perfections.—The OPERATIONS, multiplex in that they are natural or artificial[6] or moral, demonstrate in their immense variety the immensity of that power, art, and goodness which is the "cause of existence, the reason of intelligibility, and the norm of life."—ORDER, in terms of duration, position, and relative power, that is, in terms of before and after, above and below, greater and lesser excellence, manifests with great clarity in the book of creation the primacy, loftiness, and excellence of the First Principle, and thus the infinity of His power. Order in the divine laws, precepts, and judgments in the book of Scriptures shows the immensity of His wisdom. Order in the divine sacraments, graces, and just rewards in the body of the Church reveals the immensity of His goodness. In this way, order as such leads us, with certainty, to the First and Highest, to the Mightiest and Wisest, and to the Best.

15. Whoever is not enlightened by such brilliance of things created must be blind; whoever is not awakened by their mighty voice must be deaf; whoever fails to praise God for all His works must be dumb; whoever fails to discover the First Principle through all these signs must be a fool.

Open your eyes, then, alert your spiritual ears, unseal your lips, and *apply your heart*, so that in all creatures you may see, hear, praise, love, and serve, glorify and honor your God, lest the whole world rise against you. For *the universe shall war ... against the foolhardy*, whereas it becomes the foundation of glory for the wise, who can say with the prophet: *For You make me glad, O Lord, by Your deeds; at the works of Your hands I rejoice. How great are Your works, O Lord!—In wisdom You have wrought them all—the earth is full of Your creatures.*

CHAPTER II—ON CONTEMPLATING GOD IN HIS TRACES IN THE PERCEPTIBLE WORLD

1. Taking perceptible things as a mirror, we see God THROUGH them—through His traces, so to speak; but we also see Him IN them, as He is there by His essence, power, and presence. This view is loftier than the first. Thus, it holds the next higher place, as the second rung of contemplation, where we are led to contemplate God IN all the creatures that enter our mind through the bodily senses.

2. Now, the big outside world enters the little world of our soul as this soul apprehends perceptible things, enjoys them, and judges them.

In the outside world, we find three groups of things, the PRODUCERS, the PRODUCTS, and the RULERS OF BOTH.

The producers are the simple bodies, that is, the stars and the four elements.[7] Whatever is effected or produced by the action of nature's powers, is effected or produced out of the elements through that virtue of light which, in compound bodies, harmonizes the conflict between these same elements.

The products are the compound bodies themselves: minerals, plants, brute animals, and the human body.

The rulers of both producers and products are the immaterial principles. These can be inseparably combined with matter, as is the animal soul; or separably combined, as is the rational soul; or absolutely independent of matter, as are the heavenly spirits the philosophers call "intelligences," and we, angels. To the philosophers, they are the movers of the stars. They supposedly receive from the First Cause, God, a flow of power that they pour out again as required by their task of ensuring the smooth operation of nature. To the theologians, the heavenly spirits are, under God's supreme authority, the rulers of the universe in the work of restoration, and hence are considered *ministering spirits, sent for service, for the sake of those who shall inherit salvation.*

3. So the little world, man, has five senses like so many doors through which the knowledge of all that

---

[6] The term "artificial" in scholastic philosophy is applied to anything an intelligent being produces through the use of his creative mind. It is opposed to "natural," which is said of anything that results from nature's spontaneous operation.

[7] That is, fire, air, water, and earth.

exists in the sensible world enters into his soul. The brilliant stars and other colored objects enter through sight. Solid, earthly objects enter through touch. Objects between heaven and earth enter through the three intermediate senses: liquids are tasted, sounds are heard, and vapors, compounded of water, air, and fire or heat, as for instance the fumes of burning incense, are smelled.

So the simple bodies, as well as the compounds resulting from their combination, enter through these doors. Our senses do not perceive only the proper sensibles, that is, light, sound, odor, taste, and the four elemental qualities identified by touch:[8] they also perceive the common sensibles, that is, number, size, shape, rest, and motion.[9] Now, "anything that moves is moved by something else." Even though some beings—that is, the animate beings—do move and stop by themselves, when, through the five senses, we perceive the motion of their bodies, we arrive, as from effect to cause, at the existence of the spiritual principles that move them.

4. So this whole perceptible world, in its three categories of beings, enters into the soul through apprehension. The sensible and exterior objects enter the mind first through the doors of the five senses. They enter, not substantially, but by their similitude. The similitude is first engendered in the medium.[10] Then, passing through the medium, it is engendered in the external organ, thence, in the interior organ, to enter, finally, the faculty of apprehension. Thus, the originating of the similitude in the medium, its passing from the medium to the organ, and the concentration of the apprehending faculty upon it bring about the apprehension of all those external things the mind is able to grasp.

5. The apprehension of a fitting object is followed by pleasure—the senses are delighted in the object. Through the abstracted similitude, we see in the object esthetic beauty, we smell sweet odors, or hear sweet sounds, and we taste healthy foods, to speak by appropriation.[11]

All delight is based on proportion. Now, we may see in the abstracted similitude form, power, and operation. FORM refers to the principle from which the similitude comes forth; POWER, to the medium through which it proceeds; and OPERATION, to the term upon which it acts. Hence, a similitude may be well proportioned in three respects. When it is seen as containing the species or form, the proportion will be called beauty, for "beauty is nothing else but harmonious proportion," or a "certain arrangement of parts together with harmony in the colors." When the similitude is seen as containing potency or power, the proportion is called pleasantness, meaning that the acting power is rightly proportioned to the recipient, for the senses are frustrated by the extreme and delighted by the moderate. When the similitude is seen as active and impressive, the impression will be well proportioned if the impressing agent fills a need of the receiver, that is, sustains and nourishes him, which is best observed in taste and touch.

So, in the act of enjoyment, the external pleasurable objects enter the soul through a threefold delight caused by the similitude.

6. Apprehension and delectation are followed by judgment. Not only does judgment determine whether an object is white or black, for such decision pertains to the external sense, or whether an object is helpful or harmful, since such decision pertains to the internal sense, but it also determines and gives the rational explanation of why an object is pleasurable. This judging, in other words, inquires into the very principle of the pleasure the sense derives from the object. This occurs when we ask what precisely makes a thing beautiful, pleasant, and wholesome. We find that harmonious proportion is the reason. This principle of harmonious proportion is the same in large and small things, for it is not affected by size, nor does it evolve or change with the changing of

---

[8] That is, hot, cold, wet, and dry, corresponding to the four "elements": fire, air, water and earth.
[9] The perception of shape, for instance, is the result of various perceptions synthetized by what the Scholastics call "common sense." Hence the name "common sensibles."
[10] "Medium" means anything that spans the distance between the physical object and the sense organ, as space, carrying light, and air, carrying sound.

[11] "Appropriation" here means two things. First, it means attributing by analogy to the perceived object qualities that primarily belong to the perceiving subject; for instance, food is "healthy" because it is health-GIVING to man. Second, it means identifying one sense with the quality it primarily perceives, although the same quality may also be perceived by other senses; e. g., esthetic beauty is primarily associated with sight, although sound also can be beautiful.

things, nor is it altered by their successive stages. It has no reference to place, time, and movement; thus, it is immutable and uncontained, unending and entirely spiritual.

Hence, judgment is an action which, through a process of elimination and abstraction, ushers into the intellective power the sensible species first received materially through the senses. And so it comes about that the whole world enters into the human soul through the doors of the five senses by the three operations described above.

7. All these things are traces in which we can see our God. The species as apprehended is a similitude engendered in the medium and then impressed upon the organ. Through this impression, the species leads to its point of origin, that is, to the object to be known. This clearly suggests that the Eternal Light engenders of Itself a coequal, consubstantial, and coeternal Similitude or Resplendence. It suggests that *the image of the invisible God*, and *the brightness of His glory, and the Image of His substance*, exists everywhere, by reason of His original begetting, in the manner of the species which the object engenders throughout the medium. As is the species to the bodily organ, so is He united, by the grace of union, to an individual rational nature. Through this union He would lead us back to the Father as to the Fountainhead and Original Object. If, therefore, it is in the nature of all intelligible things to engender their own species, this is a clear proof that in all these things, as in so many mirrors, there may be seen the eternal generation of the Word, Image, and Son, eternally proceeding from God the Father.

8. In the same way, the species, giving delight by being beautiful, sweet, and wholesome, suggests that the greatest beauty, sweetness, and wholesomeness are to be found in that species in which there is supreme proportion and equality with the engendering object; in which there is a power imparted, not through material images, but through real apprehension; and in which there is an effectiveness, salutary, adequate, and sufficient to take care of every need of the apprehending subject. Since, therefore, pleasure consists in the meeting of an object and subject which are mutually adequate; and since in the Similitude of God alone is the notion of the perfectly beautiful, joyful, and wholesome, fully verified; and since He is united with us in all reality and intimacy, and with a plenitude that completely fills all capacity: it is clearly evident that in God alone is true delight, delight as in its very Source. It is this pleasure that all other pleasures prompt us to seek.

9. Now, judgment leads us in an even more excellent and immediate fashion to a greater certainty, as we consider eternal truth. Since judgment is based on something that is independent of place, time, and mutability, and thus of size, sequence, and change—on something, therefore, that is unchanging, unlimited, and endless; and since nothing is wholly unchanging, unlimited, and endless if it is not eternal; and since everything eternal is either God or in God: if all our certain judgments are based on this thing, it is clear that this very thing is the Reason of all things, the infallible Rule, and the Light of Truth in which all things shine forth infallibly, indelibly; without any possibility of doubt, refutation, or argument; without change or limitation in time or space; indivisibly and intellectually. Now, since the laws by which we judge with certainty all sensible things that come to our attention, exclude all error and doubt in the intellect of the apprehending subject; since they can never be erased from the memory of the recollecting subject, being always present to it; and since they are not susceptible of argument or judgment on the part of the judging subject, because, as Augustine says, "a man does not judge them: he judges by them": therefore, these laws must be unchangeable and incorruptible, being necessary; limitless, being uncontained; endless, being eternal. Consequently, they must be indivisible, being intellectual and incorporeal; not made, but uncreated; existing eternally in the Eternal Art by which, through which, and according to which all beautiful things are formed. Thus, these laws cannot be judged with certainty except in the light of the Eternal Art which is the Form that not only produces, but also preserves and distinguishes, all things; being the support of their forms, the rule of their operations, and also the norm by which our mind judges all things that enter it through the senses.

10. This speculation is amplified according to the seven kinds of numerical harmonies, through which, as through seven steps, one can rise to God. Augustine explains this in his book "On True Religion," and in his sixth book "On Music," in which he distinguishes different rhythms which gradually rise from the

sensible things to the Maker of all, so that God is seen in all things.

Augustine says that rhythms are found in material substances, particularly in sound and voice, and these he calls AUDIBLE HARMONIES. He also notes rhythms that are derived from these and received in our senses, and these he calls PERCEIVED HARMONIES. The rhythms that proceed from the soul to the body, such as appear in gestures and dance, he calls EXPRESSED HARMONIES. He sees numerical proportions in the pleasure the senses find as they turn to the received species, and these he calls SENSORIAL HARMONIES. The rhythms retained in the memory he calls MEMORIAL HARMONIES. Finally, the reasons by which we judge of all these things he calls JUDICIAL HARMONIES; these, as has been said, are by necessity superior to the mind, since they are infallibly true, and not dependent upon our judgment. By means of the judicial harmonies, moreover, there are impressed upon our mind a seventh group, ARTIFICIAL HARMONIES,[12] although Augustine makes no mention of these in his listing because they are so closely related to the judicial. From these artificial harmonies there come forth the expressed harmonies, resulting in the well-balanced forms of the artifacts. Thus, an orderly descent takes place from the highest harmonies, through the intermediate, to the lowest. And, conversely, we may also ascend by degrees to these highest judicial harmonies, beginning with the resounding harmonies, then continuing by means of the perceived, the sensorial, and the memorial.

Since all things are beautiful and in some way pleasurable, and since delight and beauty cannot exist without proportion, and proportion is first found in numerical harmony, it must follow that all things are related to number. Thus, "number is, in the mind of the Creator, the foremost exemplar"; and in things, the foremost trace of His wisdom.

Now, since this is completely clear to all, and also since it pertains very closely to God, it leads us close to Him by means of the aforesaid sevenfold distinction, and makes us know Him in all material and perceptible things when we perceive them as being numerical, find pleasure in their numerical proportions, and pronounce definite judgments based upon the laws of their numerical harmonies.

11. From these first two steps, through which we are induced to search for God by means of His traces in a way comparable to the two wings of the Seraph veiling his feet, we may draw the conclusion that all creatures of this sensible world lead the soul of the wise beholder toward the eternal God. They are the shadow, echo, image, vestige, likeness, and representation of that most good, most wise, and most powerful First Principle, who is the eternal Origin, the Light and Plenitude, and, finally, the efficient, exemplary and co-ordinating Art. They are offered to us as a sign from heaven, as a means toward the discovery of God. They are like models, or rather, things made after a model; they are set before our minds which are still uncouth and steeped in the senses; so that, proceeding from the sign to the thing signified, these minds of ours may be guided through the sensible objects they do perceive to the intelligible world they do not.

12. The creatures of this sensible world signify the *invisible attributes* of God: partly because God is the origin, mode, and goal of every creature (every effect being a sign of its cause, every thing made after a model, a sign of that model, and every way, a sign of the goal to which it leads);—partly through natural re-presentation;—partly through prophetical prefiguration;—partly through angelical operation;—partly by additional institution. For all creatures are essentially a certain image and likeness of the Eternal Wisdom, but those that are raised, according to the Scriptures, by the spirit of prophecy to a spiritual

---

[12] Cf. footnote #6.

prefiguration, are so in a special way; those creatures in whose likeness God willed to appear in angelical ministry are so in a more special way; and those things which He willed to establish as signs, and which hold not only the nature of a sign in the ordinary sense, but also that of a sacrament, are so in a most special way.

13. From all this it follows that *since the creation of the world His invisible attributes are clearly seen ... being understood through the things that are made*; and so those who pay no heed to this and fail to recognize, praise, and love God in all these things, are *without excuse*, for they refuse to be brought out of the darkness into the marvelous light of God. *Thanks be to God ... through our Lord Jesus Christ*, who has called us *out of darkness into His marvellous light*, when through these lights externally given we are led to re-enter the mirror of our mind in which divine realities are reflected.

Chapter III—On Contemplating God through That Image of Him Which Is Distinguished by Natural Faculties

1. The two preceding steps, by drawing us to God through His TRACES as reflected in all creatures, have led us to a point where we enter our own self, that is, our own mind, in which is reflected His very IMAGE. Therefore, at this third stage, by entering our own self, as if leaving the outer court, we must endeavor to see God through this mirror in the *Holy Place* or forward section of the *Dwelling*. As the *lampstand* there sheds its light, even so, the light of truth is ever glowing on the face of our mind; which is to say that the image of the most blessed Trinity ever brightly shines upon it.

Go into yourself, therefore, and behold how much your spirit LOVES itself. Now, it could not love itself without KNOWING itself; nor could it know itself without REMEMBERING itself, since everything we grasp intellectually must be present first in our memory. From this you will see, with the eyes not of the body but of reason, that your soul has a threefold power. Consider the operation and interaction of these three powers, and you will be able to see God in yourself as in a likeness. This is to see *through a mirror in an obscure manner*.

2. The function of the memory is to retain and recall, not only things present, material, and temporal, but also things at any point of time, things simple,[13] and things everlasting. For the memory holds the past by recollection, the present by reception, and the future by anticipation. It holds simple things, like the principles of continuous and discrete quantity—that is, the point, the instant, the unit—without which it is impossible to remember or understand spatial objects. It also holds the rational principles and axioms as everlasting things, held everlastingly. For memory, when co-operating with reason, could never lose hold on these so completely that, on hearing them, it would fail to approve and agree; and not as a result of a renewed perception, but through recognition of what is innate and cognate to it. This is clearly shown when we say to someone: "A proposition is either affirmative or negative," or "The whole is larger than its parts," or any other axiom which cannot be contradicted by our innermost reason.

In the first activity—the actual retention of all temporal events, past, present, and future—memory bears a likeness to eternity, whose indivisible presentness extends to all ages. From the second activity, it appears that memory is informed, not only from the outside by material images, but also from above, by receiving and holding in itself simple forms, which could not possibly come in through the doors of the senses by means of sensible images.[14] From the third activity, it appears that the memory holds, present in itself, an unchangeable light, in which it recognizes the immutable truths. Thus, from the operations of the memory, we see that the soul itself is an image and a likeness of God; which likeness is so truly present in the soul and has God so truly present in itself, that the soul actually grasps Him, and potentially is "able to possess Him and partake in Him."

3. The function of the intellective faculty consists in understanding the intelligible content of terms, propositions, and inferences. The intellect grasps the thing signified by a term when it sums up, in a

---

[13] Uncompounded.

[14] A clear instance of Bonaventure's innatism.

definition, what the thing is. Now, definitions are formulated by using more universal terms, and these again are defined by others still more universal, until finally the highest and most universal terms are attained. When these highest universals are overlooked, no clear definition of the lesser ones is possible. Unless we know what "being as such" is, we cannot fully know the definition of any particular substance. And "being as such" cannot be known without a concurrent knowledge of its attributes; that is, oneness, truth, and goodness.

But being can also be thought of as limited or complete, imperfect or perfect, in potency or in act, qualified or unqualified, partial or total, transient or permanent, caused or uncaused, combined with non-being or pure, relative or absolute, consequential or original, mutable or immutable, composite or single. And since "privations and defects can in no way be known, except through positive affirmation,"[15] therefore our intellect is not able to reach a fully logical understanding of any created being unless it is bolstered by the understanding of the utterly pure, actual, complete, and absolute Being; who is Being unqualified and eternal; in whom the rational justification of all creatures is found in its purity. How could the notion of an imperfect or incomplete being come to the intellect, if it did not possess the notion of a Being free from all defects? The same holds true for the other modes of being.

Only then can our intellect be said truly to grasp the intelligible content of propositions, when it knows with certitude that they are true; and such certitude implies awareness that our intellect is not deceived in such grasping. The intellect, indeed, knows that this truth cannot stand differently, that this truth is unchangeable. But since our mind itself is subject to change, it could not perceive this truth as shining unchangingly, except in the beam of a certain light which is absolutely changeless, and which therefore cannot possibly be created and so subject to change. Thus, our intellect understands in *the true Light that enlightens every man who comes into the world*, the true Light of the Word who *was in the beginning with God*.

Now, our intellect truly perceives the meaning of inferences when it sees that the conclusion necessarily derives from the premises. It sees this not only in necessary, but also in contingent terms, such as these: If a man runs, he is moved. Our intellect perceives the necessary logical relationship, whether the being actually exists or not. If a man actually exists, it is true that, when he runs, he is moved. The same is true even when he does not actually exist. Thus, the necessity of such inference does not come from the material existence of the object, since such existence is contingent, nor from its conceptual existence in the mind, since such existence would be purely fictitious if the object did not happen really to exist. It must come, therefore, from the fact that things are modeled after the Eternal Art. They are mutually adapted and related, precisely because they reflect this Eternal Art. For, as Augustine says in his book "On True Religion," "every true thinker's light is lit by that truth which he also strives to reach." From this, it appears clearly that our intellect is united to Eternal Truth itself, since we cannot grasp anything true with certitude unless that Truth teaches us. And so you are able to see within yourself the Truth that is teaching you, as long as concupiscence and material images are not in the way, intruding as clouds between you and the light of truth.

4. The function of the elective faculty consists in taking counsel, judging, and desiring. Taking counsel means inquiring into which is better: this, or that. But "better" cannot be used except in terms of relative closeness to "best," which closeness increases with the degree of resemblance. So no one will know "this" to be better than "that" unless he perceives that "this" more closely resembles the best. But no one will know how closely one thing resembles another, unless he knows that other. I do not know that this man resembles Peter unless I know Peter, or am acquainted with him.

Therefore, the notion of the supreme good is necessarily stamped on the mind that is engaged in the rational activity of taking counsel.

As for sure judgment on matters proposed to counsel, it is based upon a law. Now, no man can judge with certainty on the basis of a law unless he is

---

[15] That is, except by supposing the notion of a corresponding being endowed with perfection.

assured that the law is correct and that he does not have to judge the law itself. Yet our mind does judge itself. Therefore, since it cannot judge the law by which it is judging, it follows that this law must be superior to our mind, and our mind will judge by this law as by something ineluctable. But nothing is superior to the human mind except the One who made it. Therefore, in the act of judging, our deliberative power touches upon the divine laws whenever it comes up with a final and complete solution.

Desire is the strongest for what attracts the most. The most attractive thing is the thing most loved. The most loved thing is happiness. There is no happiness except through the best, and final, end. Human desire does not tend to anything that is not either the Supreme Good, or a means to it, or a reflection of it. Such is the power of the Supreme Good that everything a creature loves is loved out of desire for that Good. Creatures are deceived and fall into error when they take the image and copy for the thing itself. See, therefore, how close the soul is to God: the memory leads to eternity, the intellect to truth, and the will to good, each according to its proper operation.

5. They lead to the Trinity itself, in a way corresponding to their order, origin, and relative function. Memory begets intellection as its offspring, for only then do we understand something, when the image held by memory appears in the foremost product of the intellect, that is, in the word. From memory and intelligence comes forth the breath of love, as a link between the two. These three—the begetting mind, the word, and love—exist in the soul, paralleling memory, intelligence, and will, which are consubstantial, coequal, and coeval, and also interacting. Thus, if God is a perfect Spirit, He possesses not only memory, intelligence, and will, but also the begotten Word, and the spirated Love, which are necessarily distinct, as one is produced by the other. Since this production is neither in the order of essence nor in the order of accident, it must be personal. Therefore, whenever the mind considers itself, it rises through itself as a mirror, to the vision of the Holy Trinity, Father, Word, and Love: who are coeternal, coeval, and consubstantial, so that each exists in the others, but none is either of the others, although the three are one God.

6. When the soul speculates upon its Triune Principle by means of the trinity of faculties which makes it the image of God, it is assisted by the lights of knowledge which perfect and inform it, and which represent the blessed Trinity in a triple manner. For all philosophy is either of NATURES, or OF REASON, or OF MORAL ACTS. The first, concerned with the cause of being, points to the power of the Father. The second, concerned with the reason of understanding, points to the wisdom of the Word. The third, concerned with orderly living, points to the goodness of the Holy Spirit.

Again, the first philosophy, of natures, is subdivided into metaphysics, mathematics, and physics. Metaphysics deals with the essence of things, mathematics with numbers and figures, physics with physical natures, powers, and generative operations. Therefore, the first points to the First Principle, the Father; the second, to His Image, the Son; and the third, to the Gift, the Holy Spirit.

The second philosophy, of reason, is subdivided into grammar, which makes for potent expression; logic, which makes for sagacious discussion; and rhetoric, which makes for convincing and moving persuasion. This also suggests the mystery of the most blessed Trinity.[16]

The third philosophy, of moral acts, is subdivided into individual, domestic, and public ethics; the first, individual ethics, suggests the unbegottenness of the First Principle; the second, domestic ethics, the filiation of the Son; the third, public ethics, the distributive liberality of the Holy Spirit.

7. All of these disciplines are governed by certain and infallible laws, which are like illuminations and beams of light shed upon our mind by the eternal law. And thus, our mind, unless it is totally blind, can be led to the contemplation of eternal light by the consideration of its own self, irradiated and flooded as it is with such splendors. So this light, both as irradiating and as being contemplated, suspends the wise in admiration, while it confuses the fool who rejects faith as a way to understanding. As the prophet

---

[16] Grammar is a symbol of the Father's power to express the Word; logic is a symbol of the Word Himself (in Greek, LOGOS); rhetoric is a symbol of the winning goodness of the Holy Spirit.

says: *Thou enlightenest wonderfully from the everlasting hills. All the foolish of heart were troubled.*

CHAPTER IV—ON CONTEMPLATING GOD IN THAT IMAGE OF HIM WHICH WAS REFORMED BY GRATUITOUS GIFTS

1. We can behold the First Principle not only THROUGH ourselves as a means, but also WITHIN ourselves. Since this approach is superior to the previous one, it becomes the fourth degree of speculation. In view of the clear truth of God's extreme closeness to our mind, it might seem extraordinary that so few people should be aware of the First Principle within themselves. Yet the reason is obvious: the human mind, distracted by worldly cares, fails to enter into itself through MEMORY; clouded by imagination, it fails to turn toward itself through INTELLIGENCE; attracted by concupiscence, it fails to return to itself through DESIRE for inner sweetness and spiritual joy. Immersed in the senses, it is unable to re-enter into itself as into the likeness of God.

2. If a man falls into a pit, he will lie there until someone reaches down to help him out.[17] In the same way, it was impossible for men to rise completely from the pit of the senses to the true seeing of themselves, and, within themselves, of the Eternal Truth, until that Truth, assuming human nature in the Person of Christ, became unto them a ladder, restoring the first ladder broken by Adam.

Enlightened though a man may be by natural and acquired knowledge, he cannot enter into himself, there to *take delight in the Lord*, except through Christ, who says: "*I am the door. If anyone enter by Me he shall be safe, and shall go in and out, and shall find pastures.*" But we can never reach this door unless we believe in Him, hope for Him, and love Him. Therefore, if we want to return to the enjoyment of truth, as to the garden of delight, we must enter it through faith and hope in Jesus Christ, and through love for Him, the *Mediator between God and men*, who is like *the tree of life* standing *in the midst of the garden.*

3. So this soul of ours, this image of God, should be attired in the three theological virtues, which cleanse, enlighten, and perfect it. In this way, the image is reformed, it is remodeled after the heavenly Jerusalem, and becomes a member of the Church Militant which, as the apostle says, is an offspring of this heavenly Jerusalem: *But that Jerusalem which is above is free, which is our mother.* The soul believes and hopes in Jesus Christ and loves Him, the Word INCARNATE, INCREATE, INSPIRED, who is *the Way, and the Truth, and the Life.* When it believes in Christ as the uncreated Word and Resplendence of the Father, it recovers the spiritual senses of hearing and sight: hearing, in order to listen to the teachings of Christ; and sight, in order to behold the splendor of His light. When, through hope, it longs to breathe in the inspired Word, by this aspiration and affection it recovers spiritual olfaction. When, through charity, it embraces the incarnate Word, by receiving delight from Him and passing into Him in ecstatical love, it recovers taste and touch. Once it has regained the use of these spiritual senses, when it sees, hears, smells, tastes, and embraces the Spouse, the soul can sing with the bride the Song of Songs; that Song written precisely to train us in this fourth level of contemplation, which *no one knows except him who receives it*, since it is found in affective experience more than in rational thought. On this level, since the spiritual senses are now restored for the seeing of the most beautiful, the hearing of the most harmonious, the smelling of the most fragrant, the tasting of the most flavorous, the grasping of the most delightful, the soul is prepared for spiritual elevation by way of devotion, admiration, and exultation, conforming to the threefold lyrical outcry of the Canticle. The first expresses exuberant devotion: the soul is *a column of smoke laden with myrrh, with frankincense.* The second expresses intense and loving admiration: the soul is *like the dawn, as beautiful as the moon, as resplendent as the sun*, corresponding to the successive stages of illumination that finally suspend it in ecstatic wonderment as it contemplates the Spouse. The third expresses superabundant joy: the

---

[17] This seems to be Bonaventure's interpretation of the Vulgate's "et non adjiciet ut resurgat."

soul, *flowing with delights* of the most delectable sweetness, leans wholly *upon her Beloved.*

4. Once this is achieved, our soul has been established in a hierarchical order which enables it to ascend on high, since it is now conformed to that heavenly Jerusalem which no man enters until it has first descended, by grace, into his heart. For then, precisely, does it descend into the heart when, through the reformation of the image, the theological virtues, the delight of spiritual senses, and the ecstasy of rapture, the soul is established in that hierarchical order; that is, when it is cleansed, enlightened, and perfected.

Our soul is also promoted to nine successive ranks when within it there is an orderly arrangement of announcing, declaring, and leading; of regulating, enforcing, and commanding; of receiving, revealing, and anointing.[18] These actions correspond level by level to the nine ranks of angels, in such a way that in the human mind the first three pertain to nature, the next three to personal effort, and the last three to grace.

Having advanced through these ranks, and entering within itself, the soul enters the heavenly Jerusalem where, beholding the choirs of angels, it sees in them God who, dwelling in them, operates in all their operations. Therefore did Bernard say to Pope Eugene III: "God in the Seraphim loves as Charity, in the Cherubim He knows as Truth, in the Thrones He presides as Justice, in the Dominions He reigns as Majesty, in the Principalities He rules as Law, in the Powers He defends as Salvation, in the Virtues He acts as Might, in the Archangels He reveals as Light, in the Angels He comforts as Kindness." Thus we may see that God is *all in all* when we contemplate Him in the minds in which He dwells through the gift of His most generous love.

5. As the previous level of speculation was supported by philosophy, so this level receives its proper and foremost support from the study of the holy and divinely inspired Scriptures. Since the Sacred Scriptures are concerned in the main with the economy of reparation, they deal chiefly with the works of faith, hope, and charity, by which the soul is reformed—and most of all with charity, of which the apostle says: *Now the end of the commandment is charity from a pure heart, and a good conscience, and an unfeigned faith.* Charity is *the fulfillment of the Law,* as the same apostle also says. Our Saviour Himself declares that the whole Law and the Prophets depend upon the two commandments of love: that is, the love of God and of neighbor. These two appear together in the one Spouse of the Church, Jesus Christ, who is both God and neighbor, Lord and brother; who is also both King and friend, the Word uncreated and incarnate, our Former and Re-former, since He is the Alpha and Omega. He is also the supreme Hierarch who cleanses, enlightens, and perfects His bride, that is, the entire Church and every holy soul.

6. All Scriptures are about this Hierarch and about the mystical hierarchization of the Church, for

---

[18] This passage is more readily understood if we read it, in the light of Bonaventure's own commentary, as follows: When within it there is an orderly arrangement of perceiving, deliberating, and effecting (the natural operations of rational faculties); of regulating, strengthening, and imposing (the actions of authority); of baptizing, preaching, and anointing (supernatural actions). Cf. "Collationes in Hexaemeron," 22:25–27. In the list given in the "Itinerarium" the last term is UNCTIO. In the "Hexaemeron," it is UNIO. UNCTIO applies to the sacramental power of man; UNIO to the beatific vision enjoyed by the Seraphim.

they teach the way of purgation, illumination, and perfective union, according to the triple law they express: of nature, of Scripture itself, and of grace. Or rather, according to their three main parts: the Mosaic Law which cleanses, prophetical revelation which enlightens, and evangelical teaching which perfects. Or, better still, according to their threefold mystical meaning: the tropological, which cleanses in preparation for a virtuous life, the allegorical, which enlightens in preparation for clear understanding, and the anagogical, which perfects through transports of the spirit and the delightful perceptions of wisdom; all this, through the said three theological virtues, the reformed senses, the three levels of elevation described above, and the hierarchizing of our mind, by which it re-enters its own inner world, there to see God *in the brightness of the saints*, and, as in a resting place, *fall peacefully asleep*, while the Spouse charges: "*Stir not up, nor make the beloved to awake, till she please.*"

7. These middle steps by which we enter within ourselves, there to contemplate God in His created images, as in mirrors, remind us of the Seraph's wings spread out for flight, that held the middle place. Through them, we may understand that we are led by the hand to God's mysteries through the rational soul's own naturally implanted faculties, in their operations, relative functions, and patterns of knowledge, as shown in the third step. Likewise, we are led through the soul's same faculties in their reformed state, that is, through infused virtues, spiritual senses, and raptures of the mind, as shown in the fourth step. Again, we are led by the hierarchizing operations, that is, the cleansing, enlightening, and perfecting of human souls, as well as by the hierarchical revelations of Holy Scripture, which was given to us by the angels—for the apostle declares that the Law was *delivered by angels through a Mediator*. Finally, we are led through the hierarchies and hierarchical ranks arranged in us as in the heavenly Jerusalem.

8. Flooded with all these intellectual lights, our soul, like a veritable house of God, is inhabited by divine wisdom. She has now become the daughter, bride, and friend of God; a member, sister, and joint heir of Christ the Head; also, a temple of the Holy Spirit, faith founding it, hope raising it, and holiness of soul and body dedicating it to God. All this is brought about by sincere love for Christ, *poured forth in our hearts by the Holy Spirit who has been given to us*, and without whom we cannot know the secrets of God. *For who among men knows the things of a man save the spirit of the man which is in him? Even so, the things of God no one knows but the Spirit of God*. Therefore, let us be *rooted and grounded in love*, so that we *may be able to comprehend with all the saints* what is the *length* of eternity, the *breadth* of generosity, the *height* of majesty, and the *depth* of the justice of wisdom.

CHAPTER V—ON CONTEMPLATING GOD'S ONENESS THROUGH HIS NAME "BEING"

1. Now, God can be contemplated not only outside us through His traces, and inside us through His image, but also above us through a light that shines upon our mind—the light of eternal truth; for "our mind itself is created by Truth in person without intermediary." Therefore, those who are experienced in the first way have entered the vestibule of the Dwelling; those experienced in the second way have entered the Holy Place; but those who practice the third way enter with the High Priest into the Holy of Holies. There, over the Ark, stand the Cherubim of glory, covering the propitiatory, and through these Cherubim we understand that there are two modes or levels of contemplating the invisible and eternal things of God: one is concerned with the essential attributes of God, the other, with those proper to the divine Persons.

2. The one mode looks primarily and essentially to God's being, and says that God's foremost name is "He Who Is." The other mode looks to God's goodness, and says that His foremost name is this very "Goodness." The first approach looks more to the Old Testament, which stresses the unity of the divine essence, for it was said to Moses: "I Am Who Am." The second approach looks to the New Testament, which reveals the plurality of Persons, as when baptism is established in the name of the Father, of the Son, and of the Holy Spirit.

Christ, our Teacher, intending to lift up to evangelical perfection the young man who had kept the Law, attributes to God the name "Goodness" as belonging to Him essentially and exclusively, for He says: "*No one is good but only God.*" The Damascene, following Moses, says that the first name of God is "He Who Is." Denis, following Christ, says that the first name of God is "Goodness."

3. Let him who wishes to contemplate the invisible things of God in the unity of His essence first consider Him under the aspect of "Being," then realize that His being is in itself so absolutely certain that it cannot be thought of as non-being; since pure being implies absolute opposition to non-being, as also nothingness implies absolute opposition to being. For as absolute nothingness has nothing of being or its modes, so also pure being has nothing of non-being, either actually or potentially, either in terms of objective truth or of our understanding of it. Since non-being is privation of being, it cannot be conceived by the mind except in terms of being. Being, however, is not conceived in terms of something else; for anything that is understood is understood either as non-being, or as being in potency, or as being in act. If, therefore, non-being cannot be understood except in terms of being, and being in potency cannot be understood except in terms of being in act; if, moreover, being denotes the pure act of existence—then being is that which is first conceived by the intellect, and that very being is identical with pure act. But this pure act is not particular being, which is limited because combined with potency. Nor is it analogous being, which has the least of actuality, having the least of being. It remains, therefore, that the being we are considering is divine being.

4. Strange is the blindness of the mind, for it fails to attend to the first thing it sees, without which nothing can be known. But as the eye, concentrating on the various distinctions of color, fails to notice the very light by which all are seen, or perhaps does notice it but fails to attend to it, so the eye of our mind, concentrating on many beings of the particular and the universal orders, fails to attend to Being Itself, who is outside every genus, although He is the first to meet the mind, and the One through whom all things are known. Thus, we may truly say: "As the eye of the bat in the light of day, even so is the eye of our mind in the most obvious Light of nature." Accustomed as we are to the opacity of beings, and to the phenomena perceptible to the senses, when we face the very light of the highest Being, not realizing that this supreme Darkness is actually the Light of our mind, we think that we are not seeing anything. The same thing happens when our eyes gaze upon pure light: we think that we are not seeing anything.

5. Behold, if you can, Being in its purity, and you will realize that it cannot be conceived as stemming from another: and the very fact that it can stem neither from nothing nor from something is the reason why it must be seen as the FIRST in every respect. For what exists by itself if pure being does not exist by itself and of itself? Pure being will appear to you as devoid of all non-being, and thus, never beginning and never ending, as ETERNAL. It will appear as having nothing within itself except the very act of being, and thus, not composed of anything, as utterly SIMPLE. Since wherever there is potency to some extent, there is some lack of being, it will appear as having no potency, and thus, as supremely ACTUAL. It will appear as having nothing defectible, and thus as wholly PERFECT; and, finally, having nothing diversified, it will appear as supremely ONE.

Being, therefore, that is pure being, unqualified being, and absolute being, is first, and eternal, and also utterly simple, actual, perfect, and one.

6. All this is so certain that its opposite cannot be conceived by a mind which understands pure being, and which knows that its attributes are mutually implied. For since pure being is unqualified being, it is unqualifiedly first; because unqualifiedly first, it was not made by another, nor could it have been made by itself; thus it is eternal. Because first and eternal, it is not made of other things; thus it is utterly simple. Because it is first, eternal, and utterly simple, and there is in it no potency limiting the act, it is supremely actual. Again, because it is first, eternal, utterly simple, and supremely actual, it is wholly perfect, and as such lacks absolutely nothing, nor could anything be added to it. Because it is first, eternal, utterly simple, supremely actual, and wholly perfect, it is supremely one. For whatever is said with ALL-EMBRACING superabundance is said of all things; whereas whatever is said with UNQUALIFIED superabundance applies but to one single being. From this it follows that if the notion of God implies the Being that is first, eternal, utterly simple, supremely actual, and wholly perfect, He cannot be conceived as non-existing, or as existing in any manner other than

that of exclusive oneness. *Hear*, therefore, O *Israel: the Lord our God is one Lord*. If you behold these things in the pure simplicity of your mind, you will be filled with the glow of eternal light.

7. But there is something else here that will lift you up in wonder: pure being is first but also last, eternal but also all-present, utterly simple but also utterly mighty, supremely actual but also supremely immutable, wholly complete but also wholly immeasurable, absolutely one but also all-inclusive. Admiring these truths with an uncluttered mind, you will be touched with a more brilliant light if you note further that this pure being is last for the very reason that it is first. Since it is first, it does all things for its own sake, and consequently it must be the final end, the beginning and the consummation, the Alpha and the Omega. It is all-present for the very reason that it is eternal; for an eternal being does not proceed from some extrinsic cause, nor can it destroy itself, or pass from one condition to another: consequently, it has no past or future, but only present existence. It is utterly mighty for the very reason that it is utterly simple; for the utterly simple in essence is also the all-powerful, since the more unified the power, the greater its intensity. It is supremely immutable for the very reason that it is supremely actual, for to be supremely actual is to be pure act, and whatever is pure act cannot acquire anything new, nor can it lose anything it has: consequently, it cannot change. It is wholly immeasurable for the very reason that it is wholly complete; for if it is wholly complete, nothing better, more noble, or more excellent can be conceived, and, therefore, nothing greater: and such a thing is immeasurable. Finally, it is all-inclusive for the very reason that it is supremely one; for what is supremely one is the universal principle of all multiplicity. Therefore, this pure being is the efficient, exemplary, and final cause of all things, as "the cause of being, the reason of intelligibility, and the norm of life." Thus, it is all-inclusive, not as if it were itself the essence of all things, but as the eminent, most universal, and utterly sufficient cause of all essences; and the power of this cause is supremely infinite and multiple in its effects because it is supremely unified in essence.

8. Again, we say that, because the utterly pure and the most absolute being, which is unqualified being, is the very first and the very last, it is the origin and the final end of all things. Because it is eternal and all-present, surrounding and penetrating all duration, it is, as it were, both their center and their circumference. Because it is utterly simple and utterly great, it is wholly interior to all things and wholly exterior to them. "It is an intelligible sphere, the center of which is everywhere, and the circumference nowhere." Because it is supremely actual and immutable, "while remaining unmoved, it imparts motion to all." Because it is wholly perfect and wholly immeasurable, it is interior to all things, yet not enclosed; exterior to all things, yet not excluded; above all things, yet not aloof; below all things, yet not their servant. For, truly, it is supremely one and all-inclusive: therefore, even though all things are many and pure being is but one, it is *all in all*; for by reason of this utterly simple oneness, of this utterly serene truth, of this utterly pure goodness, there is present in God all power, all exemplarity, and all communicability, and so, *from Him and through Him and unto Him are all things*, and this because He is all-powerful, all-knowing, and all-good; and happiness consists in beholding Him face to face, as Moses was told: "*I will shew thee all good*."

CHAPTER VI—ON CONTEMPLATING GOD'S TRINITY IN HIS NAME "GOODNESS"

1. After considering God's essential oneness, the eye of our mind should be raised to behold the blessed Trinity, so that the second Cherub may be placed alongside the first. For as PURE BEING is the root and basis for the contemplation of God's essential oneness, and the name through which the other attributes come to be known, so PURE GOODNESS is the absolutely first foundation for the contemplation of the divine emanations.

2. See, therefore, and understand that the "best" is unqualified being, better than which nothing can be imagined. For a thing that is better than anything else is also such that it cannot rightly be conceived as non-existing, since to be is absolutely better than not to be. In addition, it cannot rightly be conceived except as both trine and one. Good is said to be self-diffusive; therefore, the highest good is that which

diffuses itself the most. Now, diffusion cannot stand as the highest unless it is intrinsic yet actual, substantial yet personal, essential yet voluntary, necessary yet free, perfect yet incessant.[19] Thus, in the supreme good, there must be from all eternity an actual and consubstantial producing, the producing of a hypostasis as noble as the One who produces by way of both generation and spiration. So, there is produced an Eternal Principle, who is an eternal Co-producer. And thus, there is the producing of one Beloved and one Co-beloved, of one Engendered and one Spirated. So, in all, there are the Father, the Son, and the Holy Spirit. Otherwise, this good would not be supreme, since it would not be supremely self-diffusive. For truly, compared to the immensity of the eternal Goodness, diffusion in time, as manifested in creation, is nothing but a point without dimensions. Hence, it is possible to think of a greater diffusion: to wit, a diffusion by which the diffusing subject communicates to the object the totality of its substance and nature. Therefore, good would not be supreme if either in the order of reality or in the order of reason it lacked this perfect diffusion.

If, therefore, you are able to behold with your mental vision this pure goodness that is the pure act of a Principle who loves with the love of charity, such love being both gratuitous and due, and a combination of both, such pure goodness is an absolute diffusion in both essence and will. It is a diffusion by way of the Word in whom all things are expressed, and by way of the Gift by whom all other gifts are given. Should you, then, be able to see with the eyes of your mind this pure goodness, you can also see that its supreme communicability necessarily postulates the Trinity of Father, Son, and Holy Spirit. Since goodness is supreme in them, so must communicability be; since communicability is supreme, so must consubstantiality be; since consubstantiality is supreme, so must alikeness be, which necessitates supreme coequality, and this, in turn, supreme coeternity; while all the above attributes together necessitate supreme mutual indwelling, each Person existing necessarily in the others by supreme circumincession, and each acting with the others in utter indivision of substance, power, and operation in this most blessed Trinity.

3. But while studying these matters, beware of thinking that you comprehend the incomprehensible: for, concerning these six attributes, there are other things to be considered that will lead our mental vision to the heights of rapt admiration. Here, indeed, is supreme COMMUNICABILITY together with individuality of Persons; supreme CONSUBSTANTIALITY with hypostatic plurality; supreme ALIKENESS with distinct personality; supreme COEQUALITY with orderly origin; supreme COETERNITY with emanation; supreme INDWELLING with emission. Who would not be lifted up in wonder on beholding such marvels? Yet, if we raise our eyes to the supremely excellent goodness, we can understand with complete certainty that all this is found in the most blessed Trinity. If, indeed, there is present here supreme communication together with true diffusion, there is also true origination and true distinction; and since the whole is communicated, and not only a part, the very same is given that is possessed, and that in its entirety. Therefore, the One emanating and the One producing are both distinguished by their properties, and in essence one. Because distinguished by their properties, they have PERSONAL properties; a plurality of hypostases; emanation as a manner of originating; sequence, not of one after the other, but of one from the other; and emission,[20] not in terms of physical displacement, but through free spiration based on the producer's authority: the authority which the sender has over the one who is sent. But because they are truly one in substance, they must be one in essence, form, dignity, eternity, existence, and unlimitedness.

If you consider these things one by one, in themselves, they are enough to give you a vision of the truth. If you consider them in relation to one another, they are enough to suspend you in the highest wonder. Therefore, if you desire to rise mentally

---

[19] This series is based upon the distinction between the attributes pertaining to God's essential oneness and those pertaining to the divine Persons. Here, instead of alternating the attributes in a strictly logical grouping, Bonaventure has (somewhat fancifully) modified the logical order, to accord with the terminal syllables: "Actualis, intrinseca—substantialis, hypostatica—naturalis, voluntaria—liberalis, necessaria—indeficiens, perfecta." Since such a phonetic effect cannot always be rendered in translation, the simple logical order has been restored.

[20] Not all that is said here applies to all three Persons. Emanation is proper to the Son and to the Holy Spirit, and emission to the Father and to the Son.

through wonder to wondering contemplation, you should consider them together.

4. This, too, is signified by the Cherubim, who were facing each other. And the very fact that these Cherubim are *turned toward each other, but with their faces looking toward the propitiatory* is not without a mysterious significance, later explained by the words of the Lord: *"Now this is everlasting life, that they may know Thee, the only true God, and Him whom Thou hast sent, Jesus Christ."* For we should admire the essential and personal attributes of God not only in themselves, but also in relation to the marvelous union of God and man achieved in the unity of the Person of Christ.

5. If, intent upon the contemplation of God through the attributes proper to His ESSENCE, you are one of the Cherubim, and you wonder that the divine Being is both first and last, eternal and eminently present, most simple and greatest because uncircumscribed, all-pervading yet contained nowhere, most active yet never moved, most perfect without any excess or defect yet immeasurable and boundlessly infinite, supremely one yet all-inclusive since He holds all things in Himself and is all-power, all-truth, and all-goodness—if you are, then, one of the Cherubim, look upon the propitiatory and marvel. For in Him the First Principle is united with the last to be created; God is united with man formed on the sixth day; eternity is united with time-bound humanity, with a Man born of a Virgin in the fullness of ages; utter simplicity is united with the most composite, pure action with supreme passion and death, absolute perfection and immensity with lowliness, the supremely one and all-inclusive with an individual composite man, distinct from every other: the Man Jesus Christ.

6. If, intent upon contemplating the attributes proper to the PERSONS, you are the other Cherub, and you wonder how communicability can be found together with self-containment, consubstantiality with plurality, alikeness with distinct personality, coequality with sequence, coeternity with begetting, mutual indwelling with emission—for the Father sends forth the Son, and both send forth the Holy Spirit, who is always with them and never leaves them—if you are that Cherub, look also upon the propitiatory and marvel. For in Christ there is personal union together with trinity of substance and duality of nature; there is full accord coexisting with plurality of wills, joint predication of God and man with plurality of properties, joint adoration with plurality of rank, joint exaltation with plurality of eminence, and joint dominion with plurality of powers.[21]

7. This consideration brings about the perfect enlightening of the mind, when the mind beholds man made, as on the sixth day, in the image of God. Since, therefore, an image is an expressive likeness, when our mind contemplates, in Christ the Son of God, our own humanity so wonderfully exalted and so ineffably present in Him; and when we thus behold in one and the same Being both the first and the last, the highest and the lowest, the circumference and the center, the Alpha and the Omega, the caused and the cause, the Creator and the creature, that is, *a scroll written within and without*—then our mind at last reaches a perfect object. Here, at the sixth level as on

---

[21] This enumeration is another example of Bonaventure's fondness for an externally neat and symmetrical series, in preference to a clearly logical sequence. Indeed, in the first terms of the six opposite pairs, Christ is taken sometimes as the subject and at other times as the object. He is, for instance, the subject of the unity of Persons and of the unity of accord; yet, He is the object of the unity of predication and of the unity of adoration; but He is again the subject of the unity of exaltation and of the unity of dominion. It is Christ who is one Person, with unity of accord, exaltation, and dominion. But it is we, His rational creatures, who predicate and adore.

the sixth day, it reaches with God the perfection of enlightenment.

Nothing more is to come but the day of quiet, on which, in an ecstatic intuition, the human mind rests after all its labors.

CHAPTER VII—ON MENTAL AND MYSTICAL RAVISHMENT IN WHICH REPOSE IS GIVEN TO THE SOUL THAT RISES TOWARD GOD IN ECSTATICAL LOVE

1. We have now covered these six ways of thought, comparing them first to the six steps of the true Solomon's throne, the steps that lead to that peace where the truly peaceful man reposes in the quiet of his mind as in the interior Jerusalem; then, to the six wings of the Cherub[22] by means of which the truly contemplative mind can rise aloft in the full brightness of heavenly wisdom; and, finally, to the first six days, during which the mind must train itself before reaching, at last, the Sabbath of repose. Our mind has considered God outside itself, through His traces, and in His traces; within itself, through His image and in His image; and it has considered God above itself, through a similitude of the divine light that shines upon us, and in that light itself—to the extent that this is possible in the present state of wayfaring, and with regard to the capacity of our intelligence. On the sixth level, our mind has finally reached a point where, within the First and Supreme Principle, Jesus Christ, *the Mediator between God and men*, it considers those things whose likeness is never found in creatures, and which far exceed the power of penetration of the human intellect. It now remains for the soul, by considering such things, to transcend and go beyond not only this sensible world, but even its own self. In this going beyond, Christ is the way and the door, Christ is the ladder and the conveyance, the propitiatory, as it were, placed over the Ark of God, and *the mystery which has been hidden from eternity.*

2. Whoever looks upon the propitiatory and turns his face fully toward the Crucified, with faith, hope, and love, with devotion, admiration, and exultation, with appreciation, praise, and joy, makes the pasch, that is, the passover, in the company of Christ. By the staff of the cross, he enters the Red Sea, on his way out of Egypt to the desert; there he tastes the *hidden manna*, and with Christ he lies in the tomb, apparently dead to the world, but all the while experiencing in himself, as much as is possible in the present state of wayfaring, what was said on the cross to the robber who confessed Christ: *"Amen, I say to thee, this day thou shalt be with Me in paradise."*

3. This was shown likewise to blessed Francis on the height of the mountain (where I thought out the things I have written here) when, in a rapture of contemplation, he had the vision of a six-winged Seraph attached to a cross; as I and several others were told, at that very place, by the companion who had been with him at the time. There, carried out of himself, he passed over to God, becoming a model of perfect contemplation—another Jacob now become Israel—so that, in this way and through him, God might invite all truly spiritual men, rather by example than by word, to the same passing over and the same ravishment of soul.

4. If this passing over is to be perfect, all intellectual operations must be given up, and the sharp point of our desire must be entirely directed toward God and transformed in Him. Such a motion as this is something mystical and very secret, and no one knows it except him who receives it, and no one receives it except him who desires it, and no one desires it unless the fire of the Holy Spirit, whom Christ sent to earth, inflames him to the very marrow. That is why the apostle attributes to the Holy Spirit the revelation of such mystical wisdom.

5. Since nature is powerless in this regard, and effort of slight avail, little importance should be given to investigation, but much to affection; little to speech, but more to intimate joy; little to words and writing, but all to the Gift of God, the Holy Spirit; little importance should be given to creation, but all to the Creating Essence, Father, Son, and Holy Spirit.

---

[22] There is here an obvious mistake which does not seem to have been detected by the Quaracchi translators. There is no reference in the Bible to a SIX-WINGED CHERUB. Since the present text is a summary of the whole ITINERARIUM, reference is clearly made to the SIX-WINGED SERAPH which served as the basis for the symbolical development of the work.

Let us, with Denis, say to God in the Trinity: "O Trinity, Essence of essences, and God of gods, most excellent Master of the Christian wisdom, lead us to the utterly unknown, radiant, and lofty summit of mysterious doctrine, where the new, absolute, and irreversible mysteries of theology are wrapped in the dazzling mist of a silence full of hidden teaching; a mist shining in that deepest darkness which is utter clearness; a mist in which all things shine forth; a mist that fills the invisible minds to overflowing with the splendor of all invisible and ineffable goods."

These words are addressed to God. To the friend for whom we are writing, let us say, with the same Denis: "As for you, my friend, in regard to mystical visions, with your course now well determined, forsake sense perception and discursive reasoning, all things visible and invisible, every non-being and every being; and, as much as possible, be restored, naked of knowledge, to union with the very One who is above all created essence and knowledge. Thus, in the boundless and absolute rapture of the unencumbered mind, above yourself and above all things, leaving all and free from all, you will rise to the superessential radiance of divine darkness."

6. But if you wish to know how such things come about, consult grace, not doctrine; desire, not understanding; prayerful groaning, not studious reading; the Spouse, not the teacher; God, not man; darkness, not clarity. Consult, not light, but the fire that completely inflames the mind and carries it over to God in transports of fervor and blazes of love. This fire is God, *and His furnace is in Jerusalem.* Christ starts the flame with the fiery heat of His intense suffering, which that man alone truly embraces who can say: *"My soul rather chooseth hanging; and my bones death."* Whoever loves this death may see God, for this is beyond doubt true: *"No man sees Me and still lives."*

Let us die, then, and pass over into the darkness; let us silence every care, every craving, every dream; with Christ crucified, let us *pass out of this world to the Father.* Thus, having seen the Father, we may say with Philip: *"It is enough for us";* and may hear with Paul: *"My grace is sufficient for thee";* and may rejoice with David, saying: *"Though my flesh and my heart waste away, God is the rock of my heart and my portion forever.—Blessed be the Lord, the God of Israel, through all eternity! Let all the people say, Amen! Alleluia!"*

THE TRIPLE WAY OR LOVE ENKINDLED

De Triplici Via alias Incendium Amoris

A Short Treatise on Mystical Progress, Addressed to a Priest

INTRODUCTORY NOTE

Like most of Bonaventure's works, this treatise is geometrically constructed on a trinitarian frame. In the present instance, this frame is particularly elaborate, since it combines and intertwines four major series of threefold divisions.

The basic ternary consists in the three WAYS:
> Purgative
> Illuminative
> Perfective (*Unitive*)

Now, each one of these three ways is applied in succession to each one of three interior EXERCISES:
> Meditation (*Reading*)
> Prayer
> Contemplation

The end of each of these exercises is spiritual wisdom. Specifically these ENDS are, in order:
> The repose of peace
> The splendor of truth
> The sweetness of love

These three summits correspond to the three superior HIERARCHIES *of the heavenly spirits*:
> Peace, to the Thrones
> Truth, to the Cherubim
> Love, to the Seraphim

We should always remember that the three interior exercises (*meditation, prayer, and contemplation*) *are listed in a merely logical order, without any implication that every contemplation must necessarily be preceded by prayer, or every prayer, in turn, by meditation. What the author means is that when a man meditates, prays,* contemplates, he should do so first through moral cleansing, then through rational illumination, and finally through spiritual elevation.

It is important to note that "contemplation" in the present text does not connote the mystical state of direct union with God, but the intellectual operation that consists in applying our spirit to the understanding of God, as much as our natural power permits. Mystical union proper begins at the point where this contemplation ends: it is opened by the SYNDERESIS SCINTILLA, *the "spark of discernment," which for Bonaventure is the highest possible level of natural wisdom.*

PROLOGUE

BEHOLD, *I have described it to thee three manner of ways …*, as it is said in the twenty-second chapter of Proverbs. Since every science, and particularly the science contained in Holy Scriptures, is concerned with the Trinity before all else, every science as such must perforce present some trace of this same Trinity. Hence the Wise Man says of this sacred doctrine that he has described it in three manner of ways: by a threefold spiritual interpretation, that is, moral, allegorical, and mystical.[23] Now, this threefold interpretation corresponds to a threefold hierarchical action: PURGATION, ILLUMINATION, and PERFECTIVE UNION. Purgation leads to peace, illumination to truth, and perfective union to love. As soon as the soul has mastered these three, it becomes holy, and its merits increase in the measure of its completion of them, for upon the proper understanding of these three states are founded both the understanding of all Scriptures and the right to eternal life.

Know also that there are three approaches to this triple way: reading with meditation; prayer; contemplation.

---

[23] That is, from the viewpoints of our deeds, our beliefs, and our search for union with God.

Chapter I—On Meditation, through Which the Soul Is Cleansed, Enlightened, and Perfected

2. First, let us consider what meditation is. We should know that there are three things in us through the use of which we may proceed along this triple way: the STING OF CONSCIENCE, the BEAM OF INTELLIGENCE, and the LITTLE FLAME OF WISDOM. If you wish to be cleansed, turn to the sting of conscience; if you wish to be enlightened, turn to the beam of intelligence; if you wish to attain perfective union, turn to the little flame of wisdom. In this you will be following the advice of blessed Denis to Timothy, when he exhorted him, saying: "Turn to the beam, …"

A. On the Purgative Way, and Its Threefold Exercise

3. This is how a man should exercise himself in the use of the sting of conscience: he should first AROUSE it, then SHARPEN it, and, finally, DIRECT it. He must arouse it through the remembrance of sin, sharpen it by considering the human condition, and set it in the right direction by meditating on what is good.

4. Now, the remembrance of sin must come about in such a way that the soul is led to accuse itself of a manifold NEGLIGENCE, CONCUPISCENCE, and MALICE. Almost every one of our sins and evils, those inherited as well as those committed, may be reduced to these three causes.

Concerning negligence, a man must be careful to recall whether he has failed to guard his heart, make good use of his time, or act with the right purpose. These points require the greatest attention so that the heart may be safe, time well spent, and a proper goal pursued in every deed.

Next, one must ask himself whether he may have been neglectful in his prayer, his reading, or the performance of good works. For if he wishes to yield good fruit in due season, it is necessary that he train and exercise himself with care in all these ways, since one of them by no means suffices without the others.

Third, he should remember any negligence in doing penance, in resisting evil, or in making spiritual progress. All of us should take great care to grieve over sins committed, to repel the assaults of the devil, and to proceed from summit to summit so as finally to reach the promised land.

5. Now, as to concupiscence, a man must ask himself whether there is alive in him any uncontrolled desire, born of the senses, or of curiosity, or of worldly vanity; for these are the roots of all evil.

First, let us consider the thirst for pleasure that thrives in a man who looks for sweetness, softness, and carnality. That is, one who seeks refined food, rich clothing, and lustful satisfaction. It is not only wrong to consent to these things willfully: it is also wrong not to shun them at their very first appeal.

Next, let us see whether concupiscence has ever lived or may still be alive within us in the form of curiosity. This vice afflicts the man who seeks to possess occult knowledge, to see what pleases the eye, to own costly treasures. In all these, there is the wickedness of curiosity and greed.

Third, let us consider the concupiscence of vanity, which lives or has lived in man if he ever sought favor, praise, and honor: vain things that make us vain. They must be shunned as carefully as lust for women.

These are the things of which a man's conscience should accuse his heart.

6. Concerning malice, a man must know whether there lives or has ever lived in him any anger, envy, or acrimony, that make a soul evil. First to be considered is the malice of anger, as found in thought, sign, and word; or in the heart, on the face, and in the voice; or again, in emotions, expressions, and actions. Next,

there is the malice of envy, that induces a man to grieve over a neighbor's success, rejoice at his misfortune, and be indifferent to his misery. Third, there is the malice of acrimony, whence are born evil suspicions, blasphemous thoughts, and malicious detractions. Any form of this evil must be hated thoroughly.

Thus, by means of a threefold searching of memory, the sting of conscience shall be aroused, and the soul shall taste the bitterness of remorse.

7. Having seen how this is done through the remembrance of sin, we shall now see how the sting of conscience is sharpened by a consideration of what is external to us. Man should fix his gaze upon three things: the HOUR OF DEATH, so imminently close; the BLOOD OF THE CROSS, so recently shed; the FACE OF THE JUDGE, so verily present. This threefold thought will sharpen the sting of conscience against all evil.

First, it is sharpened by the thought of the hour of death, because that hour is unpredictable, inevitable, and final. A man who sees this clearly will strive mightily to cleanse himself, while there is time, of all negligence, concupiscence, and malice. Who shall dare to remain in sin if he cannot be certain of the morrow?

The sting of conscience is also sharpened when one considers the blood that was once shed on the cross to quicken, then cleanse, then finally soften man's heart; or again, to remove man's uncleanliness, change his death into life, and bestow fruitfulness upon his barren soul. Who would be so lost to reason as to let the sins of negligence, concupiscence, or malice reign in him while he sees himself bathed in this immeasurably precious blood?

Third, the sting of conscience is sharpened when one considers the face of the Judge, for He is infallible, inexorable, and inescapable. No one can deceive His wisdom, or bend His justice, or elude His vengeance. Then, "since no good remains unrewarded and no evil unpunished," is there a man whose mind, when he thinks of such things, would not be sharpened against all wickedness?

8. Now, it remains to be seen in what manner and degree the sting of conscience is to be directed, by considering what is good. The goods on which we are to concentrate at first are the following three: ALACRITY against negligence, AUSTERITY against concupiscence, and BENIGNITY against malice. As soon as these three are attained, the conscience becomes good and straight.

The prophet says: "*I will shew thee, O man, what is good and what the Lord requireth of thee: Verily, to do judgment, and to love mercy, and to walk solicitous with thy God.*" He refers to the three goods we have indicated here. Likewise, in the Gospel of Luke, the Lord says: "*Let your loins be girt about...*"

9. We must start with alacrity, that opens the way to the other goods. Let us describe it thus: alacrity consists in a certain spiritual vigor that shakes off all negligence and disposes the soul for the watchful, trustful, and careful performance of any godly work. It is such promptness that ushers in all the other virtues.

Next comes austerity: it consists in a certain spiritual rigor that restrains all concupiscence and prepares the soul for the love of hardship, poverty, and lowliness.

Third, there is benignity: it consists in a certain spiritual taste that excludes all evil and prepares the soul for kindness, tolerance, and internal joy.

And this is the end of purgation by way of meditation, for every clean conscience is joyful and glad. Let anyone who wishes to be cleansed turn to the sting of conscience in the manner explained above—starting this meditation at will with any of the points suggested, then passing to another, dwelling upon each as long as may be necessary to arrive at tranquillity and peace. From this, in turn, proceeds an inner joy that makes our spirit ready to rise aloft. And so, this first way originates in the sting of conscience, and terminates in a disposition of spiritual joy; it is pursued in pain, but consummated in love.

B. ON THE ILLUMINATIVE WAY AND ITS THREEFOLD EXERCISE

10. After the purgative way, there comes, in the second place, the illuminative way. Here a man must learn to use the beam of intelligence in this manner: first, he must HOLD IT ALOFT to reveal the guilt

remitted; then he must BROADEN ITS SCOPE to include the favors he has received; lastly, he must TURN IT BACK to display the promised rewards.

Now, the beam of intelligence is held aloft when we carefully consider the guilt remitted by God: guilt as manifold as our sins, and as great as the damage we have incurred and the goods we might have lost. The characteristics of this meditation may be understood clearly from what was explained above.

But we are to be mindful of more than this, for we must consider also the great iniquities into which we might have fallen if God had permitted. And as we meditate with care upon such things, the beam of intelligence sheds light upon our darkness. This enlightenment must prompt us to thankfulness, else it cannot truly be that heavenly light whose glow is always accompanied by warmth. Thanks must be rendered here, then, for the remission of the sins we have committed, and for our escape from others into which we might have fallen through necessity, weakness, or perversion of the will.

11. Next, we should consider how the scope of this beam is broadened, as we behold the favors we receive. These are of three kinds: some representing a PERFECTION OF NATURE, others an ASSISTANCE OF GRACE, and others again a SUPERABUNDANT GIFT.

The favors perfecting nature are, in regard to the body, integrity of limbs, a healthy constitution, and the dignity of sex; in regard to the senses, sharp eyesight, keen hearing, and distinct speech; in regard to the soul, clear intelligence, true judgment, and proper disposition.

12. The favors representing an assistance of grace are: first, the baptismal grace by which God has erased sin, restored innocence, and conferred justification that makes the soul worthy of eternal life; next, the grace of repentance for any present needs, for the strengthening of the will, and for the betterment of religious life; third, the grace of priesthood through which you are made the minister of teaching, absolution, and Holy Communion: all these being offices in which the words of life are administered in the measure proper to each.

13. The favors representing superabundance are: first, His gift of the universe—irrational beings to serve us, human beings to be the occasion of merit, and heavenly beings to protect us; then, the gift of His Son—in the Incarnation as our Brother and Friend, in the Passion as a Price to be paid, in the Consecration as our daily Food; finally, His gift of the Holy Spirit—as a sign of acceptance, a privilege of adoption, and a ring of espousal, for He made the Christian soul His friend, daughter, and bride.

These things are all wonderful and beyond price, and the soul contemplating them should be filled with gratitude toward God.

14. As a final point concerning the illuminative way, it remains to be seen how the light of intelligence must be turned back through meditation. Man must return to the Fountainhead of all good by remembering the promised rewards. We should diligently call to mind and often ponder the fact that God, *who does not lie*, has promised those who believe in Him and love Him the removal of all evils, the company of all the saints, and the fulfillment of all their desires in Him who is the Origin and the End of all good. He is, indeed, a Good so great as to exceed every possible request, desire, or surmise; and He deems us worthy of this Good so great if we love and desire Him above all else, and for His own sake. With the full might of our yearning love and resolute will, therefore, let us press on toward Him.

C. ON THE PERFECTIVE WAY AND ITS THREEFOLD EXERCISE

15. Finally, what are we to do about the little flame of wisdom? We are to act in the following way: it is first to be CONCENTRATED, then FED, and then RAISED ALOFT.

Now, we concentrate it by turning our hearts away from the love of creatures. This we absolutely must do: for there is no advantage in such love; if there were any, it would not be substantial; and if it were substantial, it still would not be sufficient. Therefore, all love of creatures, without reservation, must be rooted out of our hearts.

16. Next, we must feed it by turning our hearts toward the Spouse. Now, we do this by considering love in reference to ourselves, to those in heaven, and

to the Spouse Himself. This leads us to realize that, through love, whatever we lack is given to us; through love, an abundance of all good is given to the blessed; and, through love, there is attained the supremely desirable presence of the Spouse. These are the considerations that set the heart aflame.

17. Third, we must raise it aloft, above anything perceptible, imaginable, or conceivable, in this way: first, looking straight upon Him whom we desire to love perfectly, we realize that this Beloved cannot be perceived through the senses, since He is neither seen, nor heard, smelled, tasted, or touched: thus, He is not perceptible; yet *He is all delight*. Next, we realize that He cannot be seen through the imagination, since He has no shape, figure, quantity, limitation, or mutability: thus, He is unimaginable; yet *He is all delight*. Finally, we realize that He cannot be conceived through the intellect, since He is beyond demonstration, definition, opinion, estimation, or investigation: thus, He is inconceivable; yet *He is all delight*.

D. COROLLARY

18. All this makes it clear that meditation about the purgative, illuminative, and perfective ways results in attaining the wisdom of Holy Scriptures. We should be concerned with this triple way whether we meditate on the Scriptures or any other subject.

He who is wise will meditate only upon these things:

—The acts of man: what man will or should do, and why.

—The acts of God: how much God has entrusted to man by creating all things for him, how much He has forgiven, and how much He has promised, these three summarizing the works of creation, reparation, and glorification.

—The principles of both kinds of acts: God and the soul, and the union that is to be accomplished between them.

Here our meditations must rest; this is the end of every thought and deed, the true wisdom where science is Life.

19. In a meditation of this sort, the whole soul must be attentive, applying all its faculties: intellect, synderesis, conscience, and will. For in such a meditation, intellect investigates and makes a proposition, synderesis judges and clarifies the issue, conscience agrees and draws the conclusion, will makes the choice and brings forth the solution. For instance, if a man wishes to meditate on the purgative way, intellect must raise the question of what should be done to a violator of the temple of God. Synderesis will answer that he must be either chastised, or cleansed by the tears of contrition. Conscience agrees: "Since this violator is yourself, you must either condemn yourself to hell, or afflict yourself with the goad of penance." Then will makes a choice: that is, it rejects eternal damnation, and deliberately chooses the sufferings of penance.

The same applies to the two other ways.

Chapter II—On Prayer, through Which Our Misery Is Deplored, God's Mercy Implored, and Worship Rendered

1. Having explained how reading and meditation lead to the wisdom of truth, we must now explain how to obtain that same wisdom by means of prayer.

We should know that, in prayer, there are three steps or stages: first, WE DEPLORE OUR MISERY, then WE IMPLORE GOD'S MERCY, and, finally, WE WORSHIP HIM. For we cannot worship God unless we have first obtained grace from Him, nor can we induce God's mercy to confer this grace upon us unless we first grieve for and confess our wretchedness. Every prayer should proceed through all these stages; since no one of them is sufficient without the others, or could lead surely to the goal, the three must be combined.

A. ON THE THREEFOLD DEPLORING OF OUR MISERY

2. Guilt incurred, grace wasted, and glory lost may each give us a reason to weep over our misery.

Whatever the case may be, our deploring must include three components—SORROW, SHAME, and FEAR: sorrow for the damage or injury; shame for the disgrace or infamy; fear for the danger or guilt. The recall of the past causes sorrow for what the soul has omitted, namely the precepts of justice; for what it has committed, namely the things forbidden under pain of sin; for what it has lost, namely life-giving grace. The consideration of the present causes shame, since the soul realizes where it is—deep in the abyss, whereas it had once been close to the summit; in what condition it is—besmirched with mire, whereas it had once been an enchanting image; what it is—a slave, whereas it had once been free. The anticipation of the future causes fear, since the soul foresees where it is headed—*to the nether world her steps attain*; what is due—a judgment, inevitable yet just; what it would receive—the penalty of eternal death.

B. ON THE THREEFOLD BEGGING FOR GOD'S MERCY

3. Whatever the particular grace we are asking for when we beg for God's mercy, such begging must stem from three things: the intense DESIRE generated by the Holy Spirit who *pleads for us with unutterable groanings*; the confident HOPE given to us by Christ who died for us all; and the eager SEARCH FOR HELP—that help we expect to receive from the saints and the just.

Desire is generated by the Holy Spirit, for, through Him, we are eternally predestined by the Father in the Son, spiritually reborn in baptism, and harmoniously assembled in the Church. Hope is given us by Christ who, on earth, offered Himself up for us on the cross; in heaven, appears in glory *before the face of God* the Father *on our behalf;* and in the Mass is offered anew by Holy Mother Church. Help is from the communion of saints; from the patronage of angels, the prayers of the blessed in the Church Triumphant, and the merits of the just in the Church Militant.

When these three conditions are fulfilled, then only will God's mercy be successfully implored.

C. ON THE THREEFOLD RENDERING OF WORSHIP

4. Whatever the occasion of our worship, three things must be done: first, our heart must bow before God to express reverence and adoration; then, it must open up to render love and gratitude; finally, it must rise aloft to the mutual delight and converse between the Spouse and the bride, as told by the Spirit in the Canticle. If the proper order is observed, the soul will find therein such exuberance of joy that, enraptured, it will cry out: "*It is good for us to be here.*" This is the final aim of our prayer; nor should we cease to pray until we reach *the house of God amid loud cries of joy and thanksgiving, with the multitude keeping festival.*

5. You induce yourself to reverence by admiring God's immensity and beholding your own smallness; you open up your heart to love by considering God's bounty and your own unworthiness; you lift up your soul to wonder by contemplating God's charity and your own lukewarmness: so that, by this comparison, you reach a state of ecstasy.

6. Know also that we owe reverence to God under three aspects: first, as to the Father who formed, reformed, and informed us; second, as to the Lord who rescued us from the fangs of the enemy, redeemed us from the prison of hell, and led us into His vineyard; third, as to the Judge before whom we are accused, convicted, and exposed: accused by the voice of conscience, convicted by the evidence of our life, exposed by the light of divine wisdom, so that in all justice, sentence must be passed against us. In the first instance, reverence must be deep; in the second, even deeper; and in the third, deepest of all. The first compares to a bow, the second, to a genuflection, the third, to a prostration. The first implies subjection, the second, dejection, and the third, abjection. We deem ourselves little in the first, least in the second, nothing in the third.

7. Likewise, we must show God our loving will in three ways: strongly, more strongly, most strongly. Strongly, by considering our unworthiness; more strongly, by considering the abundance of His grace; most strongly, by considering the immensity of His mercy. Or, again, strongly because of sins committed,

more strongly because of sins remitted, most strongly because of what has been promised. Or, once more, strongly because of the perfecting of nature, more strongly because of the clothing of grace, most strongly because of the gift of superabundance. In the first, the heart is expanded or extended; in the second, it is opened up; in the third, it is poured out, as expressed in this passage of the second chapter of Lamentations: *Pour out thy heart like water.*

8. As for delight in God, that also must be expressed in a threefold manner. First, our delight should be so well adapted to God that we must be happy to find it in Him alone. Second, we must be happy in that we please none but Him. Third, we must be happy that others share this delight with us. The first manner is great; the second, greater; and the third, greatest of all. In the first, there is gratuitous love; in the second, a love that is due; in the third, a love that is a combination of both. In the first, the world is crucified to man; in the second, man is crucified to the world; in the third, Man is crucified for the sake of the world, since He chooses to die for all in order that all may please God.

And this is the state and the level of perfect love. No man, before reaching it, should deem himself perfect. Then only is perfection attained when he finds his heart not merely willing, but intensely longing, to die for his neighbor's salvation, according to the words of Paul: *I will most gladly spend and be spent myself for your souls.* We cannot love our neighbor perfectly before we attain a perfect love for God. It is for Him that we love our neighbor; only because of Him that we find our neighbor lovable.

D. ON THE SIX DEGREES OF LOVE OF GOD

9. In order to understand progress in the love of God, we must bear in mind that man proceeds in a gradual and orderly fashion by six degrees until he reaches perfection.

The first is SENSITIVITY: that is, a man learns to *taste and see that the Lord is sweet.* And this he does by taking time out for a holiday to be spent with Him in sacred meditation; for, as is said in the Psalm: *The remainders of the thought shall keep holiday to Thee.* This occurs when meditation upon the love of God gives birth to sweetness in the heart.

The second degree is AVIDITY: that is, the soul grows accustomed to the sweetness, and such great hunger arises in it that nothing short of the perfect possession of the One it loves can satisfy it. Since it cannot attain Him in the present life, because He dwells afar, our soul constantly reaches out and overflows with ecstatical love, crying out and repeating the words of holy Job: *I should prefer choking and death rather than my pains;* for, *as the hind longs for the running waters, so my soul longs for You,* O *God.*

10. The third degree is SATIETY, which is the direct result of avidity. Since the soul, in its ardent yearning for God, is rising to the heights, anything that would hold it down becomes distasteful to it. Thus, as if filled with God, it finds no refreshment in anything below the One it loves. The man who is full and yet tries to eat more, finds in food disgust instead of nourishment. On this level of love, the soul will react in the same manner to any good that is merely of the earth.

The fourth degree is EBRIETY, which is the direct result of satiety. Ebriety consists in this, that a man loves God so much that he is not only disgusted with consolation, but even, instead of it, loves and seeks the cross. Out of love for the Beloved, he rejoices, like the apostle, in pain, abuse, and scourging. Indeed, just as a drunkard will strip himself naked without shame, and pay no heed to blows, so does the soul behave here.

11. The fifth degree is SECURITY, which is the direct result of ebriety. Since the soul feels that it loves God so much that it would happily bear for His sake every punishment and every shame, fear is readily expelled, and the soul conceives such hope in the divine assistance that it believes no power could cut it away from God. On this level the apostle dwelt when he said: *Who shall separate us from the love of Christ?... For I am sure that neither death nor life ... will be able to separate us from the love of God, which is in Christ Jesus our Lord.*

The sixth degree is true and full TRANQUILLITY. Here is such quiet and peace that the soul is, in a way, established in silence and is asleep, as if in Noe's Ark where tempests cannot reach. What, indeed, could disturb a mind that is free from the goad of craving and the sting of fear? Such a mind is at the goal, in peace and quiet; here, the true Solomon finds his rest, for *his place is in peace*.

Therefore, these six degrees of love are most fittingly portrayed by the six steps that led to the throne of the king. That is why it is said in the Canticle: *He made … the going up of purple: the midst he covered with charity*, for this peace cannot be had without charity. As soon as we acquire charity, all that pertains to perfection becomes easy: acting or suffering, living or dying. We must therefore endeavor to advance in love, for perfect love leads to perfection in all else. May God deign to give it to us, He who lives and reigns forever and ever. Amen.

E. SUMMARY

12. To sum up these distinctions in a practical way, remember that one who wishes to advance toward perfection should, by meditation, arouse, sharpen, and direct the sting of conscience; hold out, broaden, and turn back the beam of intelligence; concentrate, feed, and raise aloft the little flame of wisdom.

Then, by prayer, he should first deplore his misery, with sorrow because of the damage, with shame because of the disgrace, with fear because of the danger. Second, he should implore God's mercy, with an intense desire flowing from the Holy Spirit, with a confident hope coming from Christ crucified, and with the helpful protection obtained for him by the prayers of the saints. Third, he should render worship by displaying reverence, love, and delight in God. Let admiration for the attributes of God be like a major proposition; let consideration of them follow as a minor; and let this result in full worship as a conclusion. The man who thus constantly and intensely keeps trying, will ascend in love through the six degrees which lead to perfect tranquillity. Here, great peace is found, the very consummation, as it were, of the peace the Lord left with the apostles. Note, therefore, that in all his greetings the apostle wished for his disciples grace and peace: grace as the first good, and peace as its complement. Writing to Timothy, he added mercy, the principle of both.

Chapter III—On Contemplation, through Which True Wisdom Is Attained

INTRODUCTION

1. Having considered how, through meditation and prayer, we are to prepare for wisdom, let us now discuss briefly how we may arrive at its fullness through contemplation. For it is by means of contemplation that our spirit enters the heavenly Jerusalem upon which, according to this passage of Exodus, the Church is modeled: *See that you make them according to the pattern shown you on the mountain*. As much as possible, indeed, the Church Militant must conform to the Church Triumphant, the merit to the reward, and the wayfarers to the blessed.

Now, in glory, there is a threefold gift which constitutes the full reward: the eternal possession of supreme peace, the clear vision of supreme truth, and the full enjoyment of supreme goodness or love. Correspondingly, there is a threefold distinction between the highest hierarchies of heaven: that is, the Thrones, Cherubim, and Seraphim. Whoever wishes to attain beatitude through his merits must therefore conform himself to these three, as closely as is possible in this state of wayfaring, in order to obtain the tranquillity of peace, the splendor of truth, and the sweetness of love. For in these three the Lord Himself reposes, dwelling as in His own abode. Therefore, there are three stairs leading up to these three goals, according to the triple way: that is, the purgative way, which consists in the expulsion of sin; the illuminative way, which consists in the imitation of Christ; and the perfective way, which consists in union with the Spouse. Thus, each way has its steps, which we must climb from the bottom to the top.

A. ON THE SEVEN STEPS BY WHICH THE TRANQUILLITY OF PEACE IS ATTAINED

2. These are the seven steps by which the tranquillity of peace is attained:

One, SHAME, when we recall the four aspects of the sins committed: gravity, number, baseness, and ingratitude.

Two, FEAR, when we consider the four elements of judgment: the dissipating of grace, the blinding of reason, the hardening of the will, and the final condemnation.

Three, SORROW, when we estimate the fourfold damage done: the rejection of God's friendship, the loss of innocence, the wounding of nature, and the waste of past life.

Four, INSISTENCE, when we send out a fourfold cry for help: to God the Father, to Christ the Redeemer, to the Virgin Mother, and to the Church Triumphant.

Five, RESOLUTENESS, when we extinguish the fourfold fire of vice: aridity or sloth, perversity or malice, pleasure or concupiscence, and vanity or pride.

Six, ARDOR, when we conceive a fourfold desire for martyrdom: for the sake of perfect remission of sin, perfect cleansing of blemishes, perfect fulfillment of the penalty, and perfect sanctification in grace.

Seven, QUIET, when, reposing in the shade of Christ, in a state of happiness and rest, we feel we are sheltered by God's wings from the heat of concupiscence and the fear of punishment. This state cannot be attained without the desire for martyrdom. But there is no desire for martyrdom without extinction of the passions; no extinction of the passions without a plea for help; no help without sorrow for guilt; no sorrow without fear of the divine judgment; no fear without the memory of sins and shame for them. If a man desires to attain the repose of peace, therefore, let him proceed in the order indicated above.

B. ON THE SEVEN STEPS BY WHICH THE SPLENDOR OF TRUTH IS ATTAINED

3. These are the seven steps by which the splendor of truth is attained through the imitation of Christ: assent of reason; movement of compassion; gaze of admiration; outgoing of devotion; clothing in likeness; acceptance of the cross; contemplation of truth. Let us take these steps in order.

One, consider Who it is that is suffering, and submit yourself to Him through the ASSENT OF REASON, believing with the utmost firmness that Christ is truly the Son of God, the Principle of all beings, the Saviour of all men, the One who will repay each according to his merits.

Two, consider how good is the One who is suffering, and unite yourself to Him with the MOVEMENT OF COMPASSION, sharing the pains of the utterly blameless, meek, noble, and loving Christ.

Three, consider how great is the One who is suffering, and reach out to Him with the GAZE OF ADMIRATION for His immense power, beauty, happiness and infinity. Be filled with awe before this immense Power reduced to nothingness, this immense Beauty drained of all charm, this immense Happiness tormented, this Eternity brought down to death.

Four, consider why He is suffering, and forget yourself in a RAPTURE OF DEVOTION: remembering only that He is suffering for your redemption, illumination, sanctification, and glorification.

Five, consider how He is suffering, and PUT ON CHRIST by endeavoring to resemble Him. He suffered most willingly as regards His brother, most severely as regards Himself, most obediently as regards His Father, most providently as regards the enemy. Following His example, strive therefore to be kind to your neighbor, severe to yourself, humble before God, and shrewd against the devil's guile.

Six, consider how much He is suffering, and EMBRACE THE CROSS in an access of desire for suffering. Supreme Power, as if powerless, endures bonds; Goodness, as if vile, loud reproach; Wisdom, as if foolish, mocking taunts; Justice, as if guilty, cruel torture. You also should desire the cross: that is, a passion full of abasement by the instruments; full of insult by the words; full of derision by the sham regalia; full of pain by the torments.

Seven, consider what follows upon His suffering, and BEHOLD THE LIGHT OF TRUTH through the eyes of contemplation. Because of the suffering of the Lamb, the scroll and its seven seals were opened, as is said in the Apocalypse. This scroll contains the universal knowledge of all things, of which seven had been hidden from man, but were now revealed through the effectiveness of the passion of Christ: the admirable God, the rational spirit, the sensible world, the delightful heaven, the frightful hell, the praiseworthiness of virtue, and the guilt of sin.

4. One, the ADMIRABLE GOD is revealed through the cross, in His highest and most inscrutable wisdom, His highest and most blameless justice, His highest and most ineffable mercy. In His supreme wisdom, He has confounded the devil; in His supreme justice, He has required the just price of redemption; in His supreme mercy, He has delivered up His Son for us. Careful consideration of these things will give us a most lucid vision of God.

Two, the RATIONAL SPIRIT is revealed through the cross in a threefold distinction: in its benevolence, as seen in the angels; in its worth, as seen in men; in its cruelty, as seen in the demons. For the crucifixion of the Lord was accepted by the angels; the Son of God was crucified for the sake of mankind; and the crucifixion came about at the instigation of the demons.

Three, the SENSIBLE WORLD is revealed through the cross as being the place where blindness reigns, since it knew not the true and supreme Light; as being the place where sterility reigns, since it despised Christ as fruitless; as being the place where evil reigns, since it condemned and put to death its God and Lord, although He was both loving and innocent.

Four, the DELIGHTFUL HEAVEN is revealed through the cross as being the summit of all glory, the expression of all joy, the treasury of all wealth; for God, desiring to restore to us what had been our abode, became man, humble, pitiful, and poor. Thus Supremacy accepted misery, Justice was put to trial, Wealth assumed necessity; for the highest Ruler became a lowly slave that we might rise into glory; the most equitable Judge received the basest condemnation that we might be acquitted of sin; the richest Lord suffered the deepest need that we might abound in plenty.

Five, the FRIGHTFUL HELL is revealed through the cross as being a place replete with bitter want, vileness, shame, disaster, and misery. If, indeed, Christ had to suffer such things to erase our sins and atone for them, it is the more fitting that the damned be afflicted with them as a just retribution and repayment for their crimes.

Six, the PRAISEWORTHINESS OF VIRTUE is revealed through the cross, that we may see how precious, how beautiful, how fruitful virtue is: precious, in that Christ chose to give up His life in order to preserve it; beautiful, in that virtue shone forth brightly in His very disgrace; fruitful, in that a single perfect act of virtue despoiled hell, opened heaven, and renewed the earth.

Seven, the GUILT OF SIN, and its despicable ugliness, is revealed through the cross. Behold, indeed, what a price, what a compensation, what a painful cure, its remission required. The one Person who was both God and the noblest of men, atoned for an arrogance unique in presumptuousness, by accepting the basest of humiliations; for a greed unique in avidity, by leading the poorest of lives; for a lust unique in corruption, by suffering the most dreadful of all torments.

5. This, therefore, is how all things stand exposed through the cross, for in this sevenfold division all things are included. It follows that the cross itself is the key, the door, the way, and the splendor of truth. He who is willing to take up the cross and follow its

way, as Christ explained, *does not walk in the darkness, but will have the light of life.*

C. ON THE SEVEN STEPS BY WHICH THE SWEETNESS OF LOVE IS ATTAINED

6. These are the seven steps by which the sweetness of love is attained through the reception of the Holy Spirit: alert WATCHFULNESS, comforting TRUST, inflaming DESIRE, uplifting RAPTURE, joyful PEACE, transporting HAPPINESS, and perfecting INTIMACY. You must proceed in this order if you wish to attain perfect charity and the love of the Holy Spirit.

One, since the Spouse is at hand, watchfulness must keep you alert so that you may exclaim: *O God, my God, to Thee do I watch at break of day;* and, as in the Canticle: *I was sleeping, but my heart kept vigil;* and, again, with the prophet: *My soul hath desired Thee in the night: yea, and with my spirit within me in the morning early I will watch to Thee.*

Two, since the Spouse is faithful, trust must be your comfort, so that you may exclaim: *In Thee, O Lord, have I hoped, let me never be confounded;* and, with Job: *Slay me though He might, I will wait for Him.*

Three, since the Spouse is sweet, desire must inflame you, so that you may exclaim: *As the hind longs for the running waters, so my soul longs for You, O God!* And, as in the Canticle: *Love is strong as death;* and, again, as in the same: *I am faint with love.*

Four, since the Spouse is lofty, rapture must uplift you, so that you may exclaim: *How lovely is Your dwelling place, O Lord of hosts!* And, with the bride: *Draw me!* And, again, with Job: *I should prefer choking and death rather than my pains.*

Five, since the Spouse is beautiful, delight in Him must bring you peace, so that you may exclaim with the bride: *My Lover belongs to me, and I to Him;* and, with the same: *My Lover is radiant and ruddy; He stands out among thousands.*

Six, since the Spouse is rich, you must be filled with happiness, so that you may exclaim: *When cares abound within me, Your comfort gladdens my soul;* and also: *How great is the goodness, O Lord, which You have in store for those who fear You;* and, again, with the apostle: *I am filled with comfort, I overflow with joy....*

Seven, since the love of the Spouse is strong, close intimacy must weld you to Him, so that you may exclaim: *For me, to be near God is my good;* and also: *Who shall separate us from the love of Christ?*

7. These steps follow a definite order. There is no stopping before the last one; and the last one cannot be reached except through those intermediate, which are intimately correlated. At the first step, reason is at work; at all the following, the affections of the will dominate. Whereas, indeed, watchfulness reasons out how fitting, enriching, and delightful it is to love God, trust, as if born of it, gives rise to desire, and this, to rapture, until a state of union, tenderness, and embrace is attained; to which may God lead us.... Amen.[24]

D. SUMMARY

8. The steps described above may be summarized as follows.

First, the steps of cleansing are divided in this manner: you must blush because of your crimes, tremble in the face of judgment, weep for the damage done, beg for remedy, fight the enticements of the enemy, desire martyrdom on account of the reward, and come close to Christ, seeking shelter in Him.

The steps pertaining to illumination are divided in this manner: consider Who it is that is suffering, and surrender with faith; how good is the One who is suffering, and be filled with deep compassion; how great is the One who is suffering, and be carried away with admiration; why He is suffering, and be filled with trust and gratitude; how He is suffering, and be led to conform to Him; how much He is suffering, and embrace Him with ardor; what are the consequences of His suffering, and contemplate Him with deep insight.

---

[24] This is a reference to the usual ending of prayers.

The steps of the unitive way are divided in this manner: watchfulness must arouse you, since the Spouse is at hand; trust must strengthen you, since He is faithful; desire must inflame you, since He is sweet; rapture must uplift you, since He is lofty; delight in Him must bring you peace, since He is beautiful; joy must inebriate you, since His love is full; close proximity must weld you to Him, since His love is strong.

Thus, in the intimacy of our loving soul, let us always say to the Lord: It is You I seek, in You I hope, for You I long, to You I rise, You I receive, in You I exult, and to You I finally cling.

E. ANOTHER DIVISION: NINE PROGRESSIVE STEPS

9. The steps of progress may be divided in another way, by means of a thrice threefold distinction, corresponding to the three levels of the hierarchy. Because of original sin, three things, namely sorrow, gratitude, and conformity, are necessary requirements for any person. If man had not sinned, two things would have sufficed, that is, gratitude and conformity: gratitude for the gift of grace, conformity for the sake of justification. But now there is need also for sorrow, as a medicine, because sins committed for our pleasure cannot be erased except through painful contrition.

Now, SORROW consists in weighing the evils we have deserved by our wickedness; in recalling the pains of Christ's passion; and in trying to secure, through our supplications, remedies for the sufferings we have inflicted upon our neighbor.

GRATITUDE consists in admiration for the gift of creation out of nothingness; disregard for our own merits in the work of redemption from sin; thankfulness for our deliverance from hell. For we were created in the image of God, redeemed by His blood alone, and made free to reach the heights of heaven.

CONFORMITY consists in contemplating truth with eyes lifted upward; in extending the movement of love outward; in applying the manly act of courage inward. Thus, you must rise above yourself through a vision of the truth; and this by contemplating the divine realities through intelligence; by surveying the world around you through knowledge; by bringing judgments into captivity through faith well-formed. You must, likewise, reach out in a movement of love toward the things around you: and this by longing for the delights of heaven through wisdom; by embracing all that is rational through friendship; and by despising all carnal pleasures through modesty. Again, you must deal, by an act of courage, with the things within you: and this by attacking difficulties through vigorous effort; by performing praiseworthy deeds through magnanimity; by accepting lowly duties through humility.

10. Cleansing through sorrow, considered in regard to self, implies CONTRITION, which must be laden with grief for the evils oppressing Christ, our neighbor, and ourselves. Considered in regard to Christ, it implies COMPASSION, which must be mixed with fear because of the awe inspired by the future judgment, real though hidden, and as unpredictable as its time of coming, its day and hour. Considered in regard to our neighbor, it implies COMMISERATION, which must be prayerful and marked with confidence in the help God always extends to us by Christ, through the saints.

Enlightening through conformity implies an INTUITION of the First Truth: an intuition that is high when it faces God the incomprehensible Object, broad when it faces God the intelligible Object, and pure when it faces God the Object of faith. It implies a movement of LOVE: a love that is high when it faces Divinity, broad when it faces our neighbor, and pure when it faces the world. It implies, finally, an act of COURAGE: a courage that is high when it faces good deeds, broad when it faces the spreading of the truth, and pure when it faces contemptible things.

Perfecting through gratitude implies an AWARENESS that rises to a hymn of thanksgiving for the quality of the graces that are offered, a JOY that rises to jubilation for the value of the gifts we have received, and a DELIGHT that culminates in an embrace because of the Giver's bounty.

F. ON THE TWO MANNERS OF CONTEMPLATING THE DIVINE MYSTERIES

11. Note that our vision of truth must be elevated toward the incomprehensible, that is, the mysteries of the Trinity most high, to which we are raised in contemplation in two possible manners: one AFFIRMATIVE, the other NEGATIVE. The first is that of Augustine, the second, that of Denis.

First, through affirmation we understand some concepts of Divinity as COMMON, others as PROPER, others again, intermediate between the two, as APPROPRIATED.

Understand, and behold if you can, what in God is common to the three Persons, and see that He is First Essence, Perfect Nature, and Beatific Life. These have a necessary sequence. Again, attend, and discern, if you can, that God is Ever-present Eternity, Plenteous Simplicity, and Motive Stability. These, likewise, have a natural sequence and interrelationship.

Finally, consider that God is Inaccesible Light, Unchanging Mind, and Uncontained Peace. These attributes imply not only unity of essence, but also the most perfect trinity of Persons.

Light, as the parent, generates brightness. Brightness and light produce heat, so that the heat proceeds from both, although not in the manner of an offspring. Thus, if God truly is Inaccessible Light in whom Brightness and Heat are substance, but also hypostasis, in God there are truly Father, Son, and Holy Spirit; which are the proper names of the divine Persons.

The mind, as the principle, conceives and then expresses the word. Out of their union the gift of love emanates. This process is seen in every mind in the state of perfection. If God, therefore, is Unchanging Mind, it is clear that there exists in the divine Being the First Principle, the Eternal Word, and the Perfect Gift. These also are proper names of the divine Persons.

Peace, likewise, implies concordance, and thus more than one element. Now, two elements cannot be perfectly concordant unless they are alike; they cannot be alike unless both proceed from a third, or one proceeds from the other. But, in the Godhead, two Persons cannot proceed from the third in an identical way. Necessarily, therefore, if true peace exists in God, there must be present there the First Principle, its Image, and the Bond between the two.

12. There are three categories of appropriated divine attributes. FIRST, unity, truth, and goodness: unity is attributed to the Father, for He is the Origin; truth, to the Son, for He is the Image; goodness, to the Holy Spirit, for He is the Bond. SECOND, power, wisdom, and will: power is attributed to the Father, for He is the Principle; wisdom, to the Son, for He is the Word; will, to the Holy Spirit, for He is the Gift. THIRD, loftiness, beauty and sweetness: Loftiness is attributed to the Father, because of His oneness and power; for loftiness is nothing but singular and unique power. Beauty is attributed to the Son, because of His truth and wisdom, for wisdom implies the plurality of ideas, and truth implies their unity with the object; while "beauty means unity in plurality." Sweetness is attributed to the Holy Spirit because of His will and His goodness; for wherever supreme goodness is united to will, there are found supreme love and supreme sweetness. Thus, there is in God an awesome loftiness, a wonderful beauty, and a desirable sweetness: and here we rest. This is the elevation of the mind in the affirmative manner.

13. But there is another, and higher, approach: that is, by manner of negation. As Denis says: "(When applied to God,) affirmations are inadequate, while negations are wholly true." Negations seem to say less but actually they say more. This manner of elevation consists in using nothing but negative predications, and that in a way which is orderly, proceeding from the lowest to the highest, but which also expresses transcendence. For instance, we say: God is not perceptible through the senses, but is above the senses; nor is He imaginable, intelligible, manifest, but is above all these concepts. Then the vision of truth, having experienced the night of the intellect, rises higher and penetrates deeper, because it exceeds the intellect itself as well as every created thing. This is the most noble manner of elevation. To be perfect, however, it postulates the affirmative manner, as perfection supposes illumination, and as negation supposes affirmation. The more intimate the

ascending force, the more powerful the elevation; the deeper the love, the more fruitful the rising. It is beneficial, therefore, to practice this manner.

14. Note that on the first level, truth is to be invoked by sighs and prayer, which pertains to the Angels; it is to be received by study and reading, which pertains to the Archangels; it is to be communicated by example and preaching, which pertains to the Principalities.—On the second level, truth is to be sought by recourse and dedication to it, which pertains to the Powers; it is to be grasped by activity and endeavor, which pertains to the Virtues; it is to be assimilated by self-contempt and mortification, which pertains to the Dominations.—On the third level, truth is to be adored by sacrifice and praise, which pertains to the Thrones; it is to be admired in ecstasy and contemplation, which pertains to the Cherubim; it is to be embraced with caresses and love, which pertains to the Seraphim.

Note these things carefully, for they hold the fountain of life.

THE TREE OF LIFE

Lignum Vitae

A Meditation on the Life, Death, and Resurrection of Christ

PROLOGUE

W*ITH CHRIST I am nailed to the cross*, says St. Paul in the second chapter of the Epistle to the Galatians.

The true worshiper of God, the true disciple of Christ, wanting to conform perfectly to the Saviour of all who was crucified for his sake, should try in the first place, with earnest intent, always to carry about, in soul and in body, the cross of Jesus Christ, until he can feel in himself the truth of the apostle's words. No one will have the intimate and lively experience of such a feeling unless, far from forgetting the Lord's passion, or being ungrateful for it, he rather contemplates—with vivid representation, penetrating intelligence, and loving will—the labors, the suffering, and the love of Jesus crucified, so that he can truthfully repeat with the bride: *A bundle of myrrh is my Beloved to me: He shall abide between my breasts.*

2. Now, in order to enkindle an affection of this sort, to assist the mind and stamp the memory, I have attempted to gather this bundle of myrrh from the groves of the Gospels, which deal throughout with the life, passion, and glorification of Jesus Christ. I have tied it together with words that are few, orderly, and parallel for easy grasping; that are common, simple, and plain enough to avoid the effect of extravagance—and to foster devotion and faith.

Because imagination assists understanding, I have arranged in the form of an imaginary tree the few passages selected from many, and have disposed them in such a way that, in the first or lower branches, the Saviour's origin and life are described; in the middle branches, His passion; and in the top branches, His glorification. The first four branches have four quotations placed right and left in alphabetical order. So also with the second and third groups of branches. Growing from the tip of each branch hangs a single fruit. Thus we have, as it were, twelve fruits, in accordance with the mystery of the Tree of Life.

3. Picture in your imagination a tree. Suppose its roots to be watered by an eternally gushing fountain that becomes a great and living river, a river which spreads out in four channels to irrigate the whole garden of the Church. Suppose next that from the trunk of this tree there spring forth twelve branches, adorned with leaves, flowers and fruits. Let the leaves be a most efficacious medicine for preventing or curing any disease: for indeed the word of the cross *is the power of God unto salvation to everyone who believes*. Suppose, again, that the flowers glow with a many-hued splendor and are fragrant with the sweetest perfumes, awakening and drawing on the longing hearts of men of desire. Let there be twelve fruits, *endowed with all delights and conforming to every taste*, offered to God's servants as a food they may eat forever, being fed but never sated.

This is the Fruit born of the virginal womb, and ripened on the tree of the cross to delectable maturity by the midday heat of the Eternal Sun, that is, by Christ's love. It is the Fruit that is placed in the heavenly garden of Eden—God's table—as food for those who long for Him.

This is what the first stanza[25] means, where it is said:

> "O cross, O tree of our salvation,
> Refreshed by a living stream,
> Your blossom is so sweetly scented,
> Your fruit so worthy of desire!"

4. This Fruit is in truth one and indivisible. But because of the multiplicity of His various conditions, His dignity, powers, and acts, He provides devout souls with a great variety of consolations. Since these can be reduced in number to twelve, we describe this Fruit of the Tree of Life as growing on twelve different branches, and offer it for food as having twelve different flavors.

The soul devoted to Christ may perceive the flavor of sweetness by considering, on the first branch, the most illustrious ancestry and the sweet nativity of its Saviour; on the second, the lowly abode to which, in humility, He stooped; on the third, the loftiness of His perfect virtue; on the fourth, the fullness of His most abundant love; on the fifth, His heroism during the trials of the passion; on the sixth. His patience under severe mistreatment and insult; on the seventh, the fortitude with which He bore the crucifixion and its most cruel pain; on the eighth, the victory He achieved in the struggle with death, and in death itself; on the ninth, the wonder of His resurrection, carrying with it such amazing benefits; on the tenth, the sublimity of His ascension, from which came forth the spiritual gifts; on the eleventh, the equity of the judgment to come; on the twelfth, the eternity of the divine kingdom.

5. These instances I call fruits, because their full flavor refreshes and their rich substance strengthens the soul who meditates upon them and carefully considers each one; abhorring the example of unfaithful Adam, who preferred *the tree of the knowledge of good and evil* to the Tree of Life.

Yet no one can avoid this mistake unless he places faith before knowledge, devotion before research, simplicity before curiosity; and, finally, unless to any carnal desire or worldly wisdom he prefers the holy cross of Christ, by which the love of the Holy Spirit is nourished in dedicated hearts, and the sevenfold grace is shed upon them, as explained in the first and last verses.

6. For it is with devotion and tears that we should say:

> "Give us Your Fruit as our food,
> And shed Your light upon our thoughts;
> Lead us over the straightest roads,
> And foil the plans of our foe.
> Fill us with Your most sacred glory,
> Inspire us with holy thoughts;
> Be unto those who fear Christ
> A peaceful way of life. Amen."

A list of the chapters of this work follows.

I. ON THE MYSTERY OF THE ORIGIN

FIRST FRUIT: HIS ILLUSTRIOUS ANCESTRY
    Jesus Begotten of God
    Jesus Prefigured
    Jesus Sent Down from Heaven
    Jesus Born of Mary

SECOND FRUIT: THE HUMILITY OF HIS LIFE
    Jesus Conformed to Our Forefathers
    Jesus Revealed to the Magi
    Jesus Obeying the Law
    Jesus Exiled from His Country

THIRD FRUIT: THE LOFTINESS OF HIS POWER
    Jesus, Heavenly Baptist
    Jesus Tempted by the Enemy
    Jesus Wonderful in His Miracles
    Jesus Transfigured

FOURTH FRUIT: THE PLENITUDE OF HIS KINDNESS
    Jesus, Good Shepherd
    Jesus Flooded with Tears

---

[25] A quotation from a long poem found in many different forms in the various manuscripts of St. Bonaventure's works. Since none of these versions seems genuine, we are not translating the poem in full, but only the few lines actually quoted in the Quaracchi edition. See "Opera Omnia," Tom. VIII, p. 86.

Mystical Oposcula

Jesus, Acclaimed Messias
Jesus, Sacred Bread

II. On the Mystery of the Passion

Fifth Fruit: His Heroism in Trials

Jesus Betrayed by Guile
Jesus Prostrate in Prayer
Jesus Surrounded by the Mob
Jesus Tied with Bonds

Sixth Fruit: His Patience Under Mistreatment

Jesus Denied by His Own
Jesus Blindfolded
Jesus Delivered to Pilate
Jesus Condemned to Death

Seventh Fruit: His Fortitude Under Torture

Jesus Despised by All
Jesus Nailed to the Cross
Jesus Linked with Robbers
Jesus Made to Drink Gall

Eighth Fruit: His Victory Over Death

Jesus, Sun Dimmed by Death
Jesus Pierced with a Lance
Jesus Covered with Blood
Jesus Laid in the Tomb

III. On the Mystery of the Glorification

Ninth Fruit: The Wonder of His Resurrection

Jesus, Triumphant in Death
Jesus Rising in Glory
Jesus, Utmost Beauty
Jesus, Lord of the Earth

Tenth Fruit: The Loftiness of His Ascension

Jesus, Leader of the Host
Jesus Risen to Heaven
Jesus, Giver of the Spirit
Jesus, Forgiver of Sins

Eleventh Fruit: The Equity of His Judgment

Jesus, Truthful Witness
Jesus, Severe Judge
Jesus, Glorious Conqueror
Jesus, Radiant Spouse

Twelfth Fruit: The Eternity of His Kingdom

Jesus, King and Prince
Jesus, Inscribed Scroll
Jesus, Font of Light
Jesus, Desired End

Arise, therefore, O soul devoted to Christ, consider attentively and turn over and over in your mind each one of the things that are said of Jesus.

I. On the Mystery of the Origin

First Fruit: His Illustrious Ancestry

Jesus Begotten of God

1. When you hear that Jesus is begotten of God, beware lest some inept form of carnal thought appear before the eyes of your mind. With the insight of both dove and eagle, believe in all simplicity and grasp with penetrating gaze that from this eternal Light, both immense and most simple, both dazzling and most hidden, there proceeds a coeternal, coequal, and consubstantial Resplendence who is the Power and Wisdom of the generating Father; in whom the Father designed all things from eternity; *by whom also He made the world*, governs it, and ordains it for His own glory: partly by nature, partly by grace, partly by justice, partly by mercy, so that nothing in this world is left to chance.

Jesus Prefigured

2. When God had created nature, He placed our first parents in paradise. Later, in the severity of His divine decree, He drove them away for having eaten

the fruit of the forbidden tree. But immediately, in His heavenly mercy, He put the wanderer man upon the path of penance, and gave him the hope of pardon by promising to send a Saviour. And lest this divine condescension should remain without saving effect through man's ignorance or ingratitude, God never ceased during five ages of the history of mankind—throughout the times of the Patriarchs, the Judges, the Priests, the Kings, and the Prophets, from Abel the Just to John the Baptist—to announce and promise the coming of His Son, and to give prophetical signs of it. Age after age, for many thousands of years, He produced again and again the greatest and most wonderful signs, in order to prompt men's minds to conceive faith, and inflame their hearts with intense desire.

JESUS SENT DOWN FROM HEAVEN

3. On the sixth day the power and wisdom of the divine Hand created man out of clay. Similarly, it was at the beginning of the sixth age of mankind—when came *the fullness of time*—that the archangel Gabriel was sent to the Virgin. After she consented to his word, the Holy Spirit descended upon her in the form of a divine fire that inflamed her soul and sanctified her body in perfect purity, and the power of the Most High overshadowed her, to enable her to bear such fire. Instantly, by the operation of that power, a body was formed, a soul created, and both were united to the Godhead in the Person of the Son; so that this same Person was God and man, with the properties of each nature unimpaired.

If you could perceive the splendor and magnitude of this flame sent down from heaven, the refreshing breeze that came down with it, the consolation it poured forth; if you could understand the loftiness of Mary's elevation, the glorification of humanity, the condescension of divine Majesty; if you could hear the Virgin singing her delight; if you could accompany her into the hill country and witness how the woman who had been barren embraced her and greeted her with words by which the tiny servant recognized his Lord, the herald announced the Judge, the voice proclaimed the Word—oh, surely then, together with the Blessed Virgin, you would most sweetly sing this holy canticle: "*My soul magnifies the Lord ...*"; surely, then, together with the infant prophet, you would joyfully and jubilantly adore the marvel of the virgin conception.

JESUS BORN OF MARY

4. Under the reign of Caesar Augustus, the *quiet silence* of universal peace had so tranquilized the much-perturbed world as to permit the taking of the general census decreed by the Emperor. In the dispositions of divine providence, it came about that Joseph, husband of the Virgin, went to the town of Bethlehem with the maiden of royal descent who was then with child. As nine months had passed since the conception of the King of Peace, He came forth from the virginal womb *like the groom from his bridal chamber*; and even as He had been conceived without any stain of lust, so He was brought to virginal birth.

He who is so great and rich became for us small and wanting; He accepted to be born not in a house but in a stable, to be wrapped in swaddling clothes, to be fed with virginal milk, to lie in a manger between an ox and an ass. It was then that "there shone upon us a day of redemption in the present, reparation for the past, and happiness forever; it was then that, over the whole world, the heavens were honeyed."

And now, my soul, embrace the sacred manger; press your lips upon the Child's feet in a devout kiss; follow in your mind the shepherds' vigil; contemplate with wonder the assisting host of angels; join in the heavenly hymn, and sing with all your heart and soul: "*Glory to God in the highest, and on earth peace among men of good will.*"

SECOND FRUIT: THE HUMILITY OF HIS LIFE

JESUS CONFORMED TO OUR FOREFATHERS

5. Now, on the eighth day, the Child was circumcised, and was called Jesus. By thus offering His blood so soon for you as a price, He showed Himself to be your true and only Saviour: that

Saviour promised to our forefathers through word and sign, and like unto them in all things save ignorance and sin. For this reason, also, He received the mark of circumcision: that, coming *in the likeness of sinful flesh*, He might *condemn sin in the flesh*, and become our Salvation, and our eternal Justification, by beginning His life with an act of humility, the root and guardian of all virtues.

Why are dust and ashes proud? The innocent Lamb *who takes away the sin of the world* does not avoid the wound of circumcision; while you, a sinner pretending to be just, are fleeing from the very remedy which would lead to eternal salvation. For this you can never reach unless you willingly follow the humble Saviour.

JESUS REVEALED TO THE MAGI

6. At the time of the Lord's birth in Bethlehem of Juda, a star appeared to the Magi in the Orient, and its guiding light showed them the way to the humble King's abode.

Do not yourself turn from the brightness of this orient star that shows you the way; but rather, joining the holy kings, accept the testimony of the Jewish Scriptures concerning Christ, and defeat Herod's treacherous malice. With gold, frankincense, and myrrh, pay homage to Christ the King, true God and true man; in company with the first fruits of the Gentiles to be called to faith, adore, confess, and praise this humble God who lies in a crib; and thus, warned in a dream not to imitate Herod's pride, return to your land in the footsteps of the humble Christ.

JESUS OBEYING THE LAW

7. It was still not enough for the Master of perfect humility, who is equal to the Father in all things, to submit Himself to the Virgin most humble: He must be obedient also to the Law, *that He might redeem those who were under the Law*, so that *creation itself also ... be delivered from its slavery to corruption into the freedom of the glory of the sons of God.* Although His mother was all-pure, He wished her to conform to the ordinance of purification. Although He was the Redeemer of all men, He willed to be redeemed like any first-born son; to be presented in the temple of God, and have an offering made for Him in the presence of the just and amidst their rejoicing.

And do you also rejoice, with blessed Simeon and venerable Anna: go forth to meet Mother and Child. Let your love overcome all timidity, your tenderness remove all fear. Do you also receive the Child in your arms, and say with the bride of the Canticle: "*I took hold of Him and would not let Him go!*" Dance for joy with the most holy elder, and sing with him: "*Now Thou dost dismiss Thy servant, O Lord, according to Thy word, in peace!*"

JESUS EXILED FROM HIS COUNTRY

8. It is fitting that humility should be accompanied in a particular way by three other virtues: poverty, that is, the avoidance of wealth which feeds pride; patience, that is, the peaceful endurance of contempt; obedience, which means bowing to others' commands. So, in its lofty design divine Providence allowed that, when the impious Herod was seeking the infant King to kill Him, the Child should be taken to Egypt as a needy pilgrim, following a warning from on high. Yet, in a sense, He is killed with the children of His age who are killed because of Him; He is slain in each one of them in turn.

After Herod's death, He was brought back by divine command to the land of Juda. There He dwelt, growing in age and grace, and in His dutiful submissiveness never leaving His parents, even for a moment. Yet there was one exception: when He was twelve years old, He stayed in Jerusalem, much to His Mother's sorrow while she sought Him, and much to her joy when she found Him.

As for you, do not let Mary and the Child flee to Egypt without you. And, like the beloved Mother searching for her beloved Son, never give up the search until you have found Him. How many tears you would shed if only your, compassionate eyes could look upon this most honorable Lady, this most gracious Maiden, in her flight with her frail and beautiful Babe. Or if you could hear the sweet lament of this most loving Mother of God: "*Son, why hast Thou done so to us?*" As if she were saying: "Most beloved Son, how could You have given such sorrow to a Mother so dear to You, and one who loves You so much?"

THIRD FRUIT: THE LOFTINESS OF HIS POWER

JESUS, HEAVENLY BAPTIST

9. When the Saviour reached the age of thirty, designing now to bring about the actual work of salvation, He first acted, then taught. Starting with the first sacrament, the foundation of all virtues, He wished to be baptized by John so as to give an example of perfect justification, and as if to impart to water, through the touch of His most pure flesh, the power of regeneration.

It is for you also to remain faithfully by His side. Once regenerated in Him, delve into His secrets, so that "on the banks of the River Jordan you may know the Father in the Voice, the Son in the Flesh, and the Holy Spirit in the Dove; and, the heaven of the Trinity being open to you," you may be carried up to God.

JESUS TEMPTED BY THE ENEMY

10. *Then Jesus was led into the desert by the Spirit, to be tempted by the devil*, so that by humbly tolerating the enemy's attack, He might make us humble, and by overcoming him, He might make us strong. He firmly embraced a hard and solitary life in order to prompt the faithful to embrace perfection courageously, and to strengthen them in preparation for the bearing of heavy burdens to the end.

So now, disciple of Christ, penetrate with your good Master the secrets of solitude. Once you have become, as it were, a companion of the wild beasts, imitate and share the mysterious struggle with a cunning enemy, and learn to have recourse to Christ in the critical moments of temptation: *for we have not a high priest who cannot have compassion on our infirmities, but One tried as we are in all things, except sin.*

JESUS, WONDERFUL IN HIS MIRACLES

11. He is the Lord *who alone does wondrous deeds*; who changes material substances, multiplies the loaves, walks on the waters and calms the waves; who restrains the demons and drives them to flight; who cures the sick, cleanses the lepers, and raises the dead; who makes the blind to see, the deaf to hear, and the lame to walk; who restores sensation and motion to the palsied and the withered.

Our sinful conscience cries out to Him, now with the faithful leper: "*Lord, if Thou wilt, Thou canst make me clean*"; now with the centurion: "*Lord, my servant is lying sick in the house, paralyzed, and is grievously afflicted*"; again, with the woman of Canaan: "*Have pity on me, O Lord, Son of David*"; with the woman suffering from hemorrhage: "*If I touch but His cloak, I shall be saved*"; and with Mary and Martha: "*Lord, behold, he whom Thou lovest is sick.*"

JESUS TRANSFIGURED

12. Intending to strengthen the human soul with the hope of eternal reward, *Jesus took Peter, James, and his brother John, and led them up a high mountain.* There, He revealed to them the mystery of the Trinity, foretold the humiliation of His passion, and showed them, through His transfiguration, the glory of His future resurrection. The Law and the Prophets bore witness to Him in the apparition of Moses and Elias; the Father and the Holy Spirit bore witness also, manifest as a Voice and a Cloud. And truly the soul devoted to Him, now solidly established in the truth and raised to the summit of virtue, could make Peter's words its own and exclaim with him: "*Lord, it is good for us to be here*"—here, that is, in the peace and joy of seeing Your face; here, where the spirit, in a state of heavenly and ecstatic rapture, can hear *secret words that man may not repeat.*

FOURTH FRUIT: THE PLENITUDE OF HIS KINDNESS

JESUS, GOOD SHEPHERD

13. How great was this loving Shepherd's solicitous care for the lost sheep, and how great His mercy, the Good Shepherd Himself explains figuratively in the parable of the hundredth sheep which was lost, then finally found and brought back on the joyful Shepherd's shoulder. "*The Good Shepherd,*" He says, "*lays down His life for His sheep.*" In Him the words of the prophet are perfectly fulfilled: "*He shall feed His flock like a shepherd.*" To do this, He suffered much in labors, anxiety, and need. He traveled through towns and villages announcing the kingdom of God, in spite of many dangers and the plotting of the Pharisees. He spent nights in watchful prayer. Unafraid of Pharisaical censure and false scandal, He was kind to the publicans, saying that He had come into the world for the sake of those who were sick. He also displayed a paternal affection for the repentant, showing them the open arms of divine mercy. As witnesses to this, we may call upon and summon Matthew, Zacchaeus, the sinful woman who cast herself down at His feet, and the woman taken in adultery.

Follow closely, therefore, this Shepherd most kind, as Matthew did; receive Him into your home, as did Zacchaeus; anoint Him with perfume, wash His feet with tears, wipe them with your hair, and cover them with kisses, so that at the end you may deserve, like the woman brought to Him for judgment, to hear the sentence of forgiveness: "*Has no one condemned thee?... Neither will I condemn thee. Go thy way, and from now on sin no more.*"

JESUS FLOODED WITH TEARS

14. To pour out the sweetness of a supreme love, Jesus, source of all mercy, sorrowed for us wretched creatures, not once but many times. First, over Lazarus, then over the City, and finally on the cross,[26] He wept, the tears streaming forth from His loving eyes in expiation of all sins. Abundantly the Saviour wept, deploring in the first instance the misery of human weakness, then the darkness of blinded hearts, finally the depravity of obdurate malice.

O stubborn heart, insane and irreverent, pitiable because devoid of true life, why is it that in your misery you laugh and rejoice like a madman, while the Wisdom of the Father weeps over you? Behold the grief of Him who brings you healing, and *make thee mourning as for an only son, a bitter lamentation.— Let tears run down like a torrent day and night: give thyself no rest, and let not the apple of thy eye cease.*

JESUS, ACCLAIMED MESSIAS

15. After the raising of Lazarus, after the anointing of Jesus with a jarful of perfume, as the fragrance of His fame had since long spread out among the people, the Lord, knowing that a crowd was to meet Him, went to them mounted on an ass so that, amid the very applause of these men who threw palms and strewed their garments before Him, He gave a wonderful example of humility. And even while the crowds were singing His praise, He was lamenting over the fall of the City, moved, as ever, by compassion.

Arise now, O handmaid of the Saviour, and like a daughter of Jerusalem behold King Solomon in the honor which Mother Synagogue reverently offered Him as a mystical sign of the birth of the Church. And with your works of piety and the victories of your virtues, as with so many olive branches and palms, always follow Him who is riding a lowly beast— follow the Lord of heaven and earth.

JESUS, SACRED BREAD

16. Among all the memorable events of Christ's life, the most worthy of special remembrance is the Last Supper. At this sacred feast there was offered for

---

[26] There seems to be no scriptural text supporting an actual shedding of tears on the cross, but there is no doubt about Christ's sorrow for man's obdurate malice.

food, not only the paschal lamb, but also the Immaculate Lamb Himself *who takes away the sin of the world*; who, under the appearance of bread *endowed with all delights and conforming to every taste*, is given as nourishment. Wondrously glowed the tender love of Christ at this feast, as He sat at the same table and shared the same dish with the humble apostles—even with the traitor Judas. Stupendous was the example of humility when the King of Glory, girt with a towel, stooped to the task of washing the feet of the fishermen—even the feet of His betrayer. Illimitably rich was the generosity He showed when He gave His very Body and Blood as food and drink to these first priests. For, giving to them, He gave to the whole Church and the whole world; so that what was to be in the near future a sacrifice pleasing to God and the priceless price of our redemption would also become viaticum and sustenance for men. Intense past comprehension, finally, did His love show itself to be when, loving His own to the end, He steadied them in virtue with gentle, heart-lifting words, warning Peter in particular to be strong in faith, and letting John lean upon His holy breast.

How wonderful are these prodigies of love, how full of delight—but only to the one who, called to such a solemn feast, will hurry there with all the ardor of his heart, crying out with the prophet: "*As the hind longs for the running waters, so my soul longs for You, O God!*"

II. On the Mystery of the Passion

Fifth Fruit: His Heroism in Trials

Jesus Betrayed by Guile

17. The first thing that occurs to the mind of anyone who would contemplate devoutly the passion of Christ is the perfidy of the traitor. This man was so filled with the poison of deceit that he would betray his Master and Lord; he burned so intensely with the fire of greed that he would sell for money the All-good God, and accept for Christ's priceless Blood the price of a cheap reward; he was so ungrateful that he would pursue to death the One who had entrusted the common purse to him, and had elevated him to the dignity of apostleship; he was so hard of heart that neither the intimacy of the supper, nor the humble service rendered by Christ, nor the sweetness of Christ's words, could change his evil mind. Oh, sublime goodness of the Master toward a servant so full of iniquity! Truly, *it were better for that man if he had not been born.*

But however deep the traitor's impiety, the most sweet meekness of the Lamb of God was immeasurably deeper. This meekness was given as an example to mankind, so that when we are hurt by a friend, we may say no more in our human weakness: "*If an enemy had reviled me, I could have borne it.*" For here is another self, a companion and bosom friend, who partook of the bread of Christ, and shared the divine food at this sacred supper: and he it is who has raised his heel against Him! Yet, at the very hour of the betrayal, this Lamb most mild did not refuse to the lips full of malice the sweet kiss of His mouth in which no deceit was found. He wished to offer Judas every opportunity to change his obdurate heart.

Jesus Prostrate in Prayer

18. *Jesus, therefore, knowing all that was to come upon Him* in accordance with the secret dispositions of the Most High, led His apostles in the recitation of a hymn and went out to Mount Olivet. There he prayed to His Father, as was His custom; but at this particular moment, with the agony of death approaching, with the flock which the gentle Shepherd had so tenderly nurtured about to be scattered and left without a leader, the vision of death became so frightening to Christ's sensible nature that He cried out: "*Father, if it is possible, let this cup pass away from Me!*" And the intensity of the anguish that for many reasons pressed upon the Redeemer's spirit is shown by the sweat of blood which so abundantly ran to the ground from every pore of His body.

"O mighty Lord Jesus, whence such torment in Your soul? Why such an anguished plea? Did You not offer to the Father an entirely willing sacrifice?"

It was to strengthen us in faith by the knowledge that You did truly share our mortal nature; to lift us up in hope when we ourselves must endure hardships; and to give us greater incentives to love You—it was for these reasons that You showed the natural weakness of the flesh by such evident signs; making us understand how truly You have *carried our sorrows*, how really Your senses suffered from the bitterness of Your passion.

JESUS SURROUNDED BY THE MOB

19. Yet, when the *men of blood*, led by the betrayer, came in the night with torches, lanterns, and weapons to capture Him, He clearly showed His readiness. He hurried forward to meet them, proclaimed His identity, and gave Himself up. Even so, in order that human presumption might realize it is powerless against Him except as He permits, He caused these servants of evil to fall to the ground by a word expressing His almighty power. But not even then did He *in anger withhold His compassion*, nor did this honeycomb cease to drip loving-kindness: for He healed with a touch of His hand the ear of the arrogant servant, severed by one of His disciples, and He restrained the zeal of His defender, bent on wounding the aggressors.

Cursed be their fury because it is violent: for neither miraculous might nor wonder-working kindness could restrain it.

JESUS TIED WITH BONDS

20. Finally, who could hear without sorrow of the fierce executioners laying their murderous hands upon the King of Glory at that hour, tying with bonds the innocent hands of the gentle Christ, and shamefully dragging to the sacrifice the Lamb most meek and silent, as if He were a criminal? What a shaft of pain must have pierced the hearts of the disciples as they saw their beloved Master and Lord betrayed by one of their company, and led away toward His death with His hands bound behind Him like an evildoer. It was then that the impious Judas himself, driven by remorse, became so filled with self-loathing that he preferred death to life. Yet woe to the man who lost the hope of being forgiven even then—who, terror-stricken by the enormity of his crime, gave up to despair instead of returning, even then, to the Source of all mercy.

SIXTH FRUIT: HIS PATIENCE UNDER MISTREATMENT

JESUS DENIED BY HIS OWN

21. When the shepherd is captured, the sheep of the flock scatter far and wide. The Master is seized, and the disciples flee. Peter, somewhat more faithful than the others, *was following Him at a distance, even to the courtyard of the high priest*; but there, questioned by a maidservant, he denied three times with an oath that he had ever known Christ. When, finally, the cock crowed, and the kind Master looked upon His chosen disciple with pity and forgiveness, Peter, now remembering the earlier warning, *went out and wept bitterly*.

You souls who at the word of a petulant servant—that is, your own flesh—have ever shamelessly denied by thought or deed the Christ who suffered for you: go out, all of you, with Peter! Remembering the passion of the beloved Master, weep bitterly over yourself, when the One who looked upon the weeping Peter deigns to look upon you also. Be inebriated with the *wormwood* of a bitter twofold sadness: remorse for your sins, and compassion for Christ. Then, relieved like Peter of the guilt of your crime, you may like Peter be filled with the spirit of holiness.

JESUS BLINDFOLDED

22. Led before the council of the evil-minded high priests, our High Priest Jesus Christ bore witness to the truth that He was the Son of God. Thereupon He was condemned to death as if for blasphemy, and endured much shameless infamy.

His face, worthy of the elders' reverence and the angels' desire, His face which fills the heavens with joy, was defiled by spittle from impure lips, struck by impious and sacrilegious hands, and covered in derision with a veil. The Lord of all creation suffered blows as if He were a lowly slave. Yet His countenance remained quiet and humble as He mildly and justly reproved the high priest's servant who had struck Him: "*If I have spoken ill, bear witness to the evil; but if well, why dost thou strike Me?*"

O Jesus truthful and kind, how could any soul that loves You, beholding such a sight and hearing such insults, still restrain her tears and hide her inner compassion?

JESUS DELIVERED TO PILATE

23. Oh, horrible impiety of the Jewish mob that, not content with inflicting upon Him insults innumerable, went on, convulsed with animal rage, to abandon the life of the Just One to a pagan judge, throwing Him, as it were, to a mad dog's fangs. For the priests dragged the fettered Christ before Pilate, and clamored for the crucifixion of Him *who knew nothing of sin.* While He stood there quiet and meek before His judge, *as a lamb before his shearer*, liars and evil men flung a mass of false accusations against Him. They shouted tumultuously for the death of the Author of life, while they saved the life of a murderer and seditious thief. With a folly equal to their wickedness, they preferred the wolf to the Lamb, death to Life, darkness to Light.

O sweet Jesus, who could be so pitiless as not to cry out and groan in spirit while hearing, or considering in his mind, those horrible cries: "*Away with Him! Away with Him! Crucify Him!*"

JESUS CONDEMNED TO DEATH

24. Pilate was fully aware that it was not for the sake of justice, but out of the depth of their hatred, that the Jews were thus frenzied against Jesus; he publicly admitted that he could find in Him nothing deserving of death. Yet he yielded to human fear, hardened his heart, and delivered the All-Good King to the judgment of the cruel tyrant Herod. And when Herod, after making public sport of the Innocent One, had sent Him back, Pilate gave an even more brutal order. Christ was stripped before the mocking soldiers, so that the savage scourgers could atrociously lash and tear this virginal and most pure flesh, fiercely inflicting stripe upon stripe, wound upon wound. From the torn flesh of the utterly innocent and loving One, in whom no guilt whatever had been found, the precious blood ran freely down.

And you, man of perdition, chief cause of all this suffering and sorrow, how is it that you do not break down and weep? See the spotless Lamb choosing to be condemned by an unjust sentence for your sake; to save you from the just sentence of damnation. See Him paying back for your sake what He did not steal; while you, my impious and wicked soul, do not pay Him even due homage of grateful devotion, nor offer Him the compassion of your heart.

SEVENTH FRUIT: HIS FORTITUDE UNDER TORTURE

JESUS DESPISED BY ALL

25. Pilate then pronounced the judgment agreeable to the demands of the wicked. The sacrilegious soldiers were not content to crucify the Saviour: they must first humiliate Him to the soul with the shame of mockery. *They gathered together about Him the whole cohort. And they stripped Him and put on Him a scarlet cloak; and plaiting a crown*

of thorns, they put it upon His head, and a reed in His right hand; and bending the knee before Him, they mocked Him ... and they spat on Him, and took the reed and kept striking Him on the head.

Attend now, O pride of the human heart that shuns humiliation and craves distinction! Who is this man clothed in the trappings of royalty, that He may be loaded with disgrace like a contemptible slave? He is your King and your God. He was held to be *as it were a leper* and *the most abject of men* in order to save you from eternal abjection, and to deliver you from the curse of pride. Woe, and woe again, to those who behold this utter lowliness, and yet exalt themselves in their pride; *they crucify again for themselves the Son of God*, who has deserved the homage of men in the measure that He suffered humiliation for their sake.

JESUS NAILED TO THE CROSS

26. When these godless men finally tired of mocking the meekest of kings, they returned His garments, of which He would soon be despoiled again. *And bearing the cross for Himself, He went forth to the place called the Skull*. There they stripped Him to the skin, covering Him only with a poor loincloth. They threw Him roughly upon the wood of the cross, and pushed, and pulled, and dragged, and stretched Him back and forth as they would stretch a hide. They pierced Him with sharp nails, attaching His cruelly lacerated body to the cross by His hands and feet. His garments, given to them as spoil, were divided into shares—all except His seamless robe, which was not divided, but went by lot to one of them.

And now, my soul, consider how the One *who is, over all things, God blessed forever*, is submerged in a flood of suffering *from the sole of the foot unto the top of the head*. He permits the waters of affliction to flow even unto His soul, in order to save you from all such afflictions. He is crowned with thorns; He is forced to stoop under the load of the cross, bearing the instrument of His own disgrace; He is led to the place of execution and stripped of His clothes, so that the scourge-inflicted bruises and wounds, exposed on the back and the sides of His body, make Him appear like a leper. Then, He is transfixed with the nails. All to show that He is your Beloved, martyred wound by wound for the sake of your healing.

Oh, that I might have my request, and that God would grant what I long for, so that in my whole being, mind and body, I might be pierced, and attached with my Beloved to the gibbet of the cross!

JESUS LINKED WITH ROBBERS

27. As a further addition of shame, disgrace, and infamy, while His friends weep and His enemies jeer, the Innocent Lamb is offered as a public spectacle and lifted up on a cross between robbers; at noontime; on a solemn vigil; in a place outside the city gate reserved for the punishment of criminals. *Now the passers-by were ... shaking their heads*, and those who stood by the cross were shouting and asking why He, the Saviour of others, could not save Himself. Even while one of the robbers shared in the mockeries, the Lamb most mild was praying with sweet kindness to the Father in behalf of those who were crucifying and deriding Him. In His most generous love, He promised paradise to the other robber, who confessed His Kingship and begged His mercy. Oh, words full of sweetness and pardon: "*Father, forgive them, for they do not know what they are doing!*" Oh, words full of love and grace: "*This day thou shalt be with Me in paradise!*"

Take courage and hope for pardon, O soul, however great your sins, if you are ready to follow in the footsteps of the Lord God who is suffering for you; "who, throughout His torments, did not once open His mouth to utter the slightest word of complaint or self-defense, of threat or condemnation against those accursed dogs. Instead, He poured upon His enemies the words of a new blessing the like of which had not been heard since the world began." Say, therefore, with great confidence: "*Have pity on me, O God; have pity on me, for in You I take refuge*," in order that at the time of your death you may hear, like the repentant thief: "*This day thou shalt be with Me in paradise!*"

JESUS MADE TO DRINK GALL

28. *After this, Jesus, knowing that all things were now accomplished, that the Scripture might be fulfilled said, "I thirst."* John, an eyewitness, tells us that after a drink of vinegar and gall was given to Jesus on a sponge, He said, "*It is consummated*"; as if with the taste of vinegar and gall, the fullness of His bitter suffering had been achieved.[27] It was through tasting the sweetness of the forbidden fruit that Adam the sinner became the cause of our whole perdition; it was suitable and fitting, then, that our saving remedy should be found in the exact opposite. As the deadly darts of extreme suffering multiplied in Christ's every limb, and His spirit drank in their poison, it was fitting that the mouth and the tongue—organs of nutrition and expression—be not spared either. For the prophet's words, *he hath filled Me with bitterness, he hath inebriated Me with wormwood*, were to be fulfilled in Him who is our Healing; and these further words, *He hath made Me desolate, wasted with sorrow all the day long*, in His loving Mother.

O Virgin blest, what tongue could utter, what mind could grasp, the heaviness of your sorrow! You were present at all these events, standing close by and taking part in them in every possible way. This sacred and most holy flesh you had so chastely conceived, so tenderly nourished and sustained with your milk, so often held in your arms and kissed with your lips, so often gazed upon with your bodily eyes, you now see torn by the blows of the scourging, then pierced with the barbs of the thorns, then struck with a reed, then battered by hands and fists, then transfixed with nails, then attached to the wood of the cross and opened with a spear, then mocked in all possible ways, and, finally, made to drink vinegar and gall!

But, with the eyes of the mind, you beheld also this divine soul filled with the gall of every bitterness. You saw Him, now trembling in foreknowledge, now filled with fear and weariness, now in the throes of agony, now anguished, now moved to the depth of His being, now oppressed by the most dreadful sorrow and pain; partly because of the acuteness of bodily torment, partly out of zeal for the divine honor outraged by sin, partly through pity for the wretched sinners. And it was partly also through compassion for you, O sweetest Mother, when He looked upon you with tender eyes as you stood before Him, your innermost heart pierced with a sword of grief, and said lovingly: "*Woman, behold, thy son*"—thus to comfort your heart in its pain; for He knew that your heart was more severely wounded by the sword of compassion for Him than if you had suffered in your own body.

EIGHTH FRUIT: HIS VICTORY OVER DEATH

JESUS, SUN DIMMED IN DEATH

29. Finally, after the innocent Lamb, the true Sun of Justice, had been hanging for three hours upon the cross, while the visible sun, out of compassion for its Maker, was hiding the rays of its light, the Fountain of Life itself dries up. At the ninth hour, all being now fulfilled, Jesus, God and man, *with a loud cry and tears* to manifest the mercy of His heart and declare the might of His divinity, commends His soul into the hands of the Father, and expires. Then, *the curtain of the temple was torn in two from top to bottom; and the earth quaked, and the rocks were rent, and the tombs were opened*. Then, the centurion recognized Him as veritable God. Then, those who had come to see the spectacle and jeer *began to return beating their breasts*. Then, the One who is *fairer in beauty … than the sons of men*, with His eyes clouding and His cheeks growing pale, became ugly for the sake of the sons of men, even as He became a fragrant holocaust offered for the Father's glory, to turn the divine anger from us.

O Lord, Father all-holy, *look down, then, from heaven, Your holy abode;—look upon the face of Your Anointed*; behold, Father, this most holy Sacrifice that our High Priest offers You for our sins;

---

[27] The modern interpretation seems to be that vinegar and gall were given, not as a further punishment, but as an anesthetic to dull the pain of the crucified.

let Your blazing wrath die down; relent in punishing Your people.

And you, redeemed man—see who is hanging for you on the cross; how great He is whose death revives the dead. Here heaven and earth lament and the hardest rocks split apart as if by natural compassion. O human heart, if you are not stricken with terror, moved with pity, riven with sorrow, softened with love, at the sight of such atonement, you are harder than the hardest rock.

JESUS PIERCED WITH A LANCE

30. That the Church might be formed out of the side of Jesus, inert upon the cross, and that the words of Scripture, *They shall look upon Him whom they have pierced*, might be fulfilled, divine disposition permitted that one of the soldiers thrust a lance into His sacred side. It opened up a flow of blood mixed with water which ran freely as the price of our salvation; gushing forth from the inner fountain of the heart to provide the sacraments of the Church with abundant power for conferring a life of grace, and to become, for those already alive in Christ, the draught of living water.

Behold how the spear thrown by the perfidy of Saul—that is, of the rejected Jewish people—is by divine mercy fastened in the wall of His side, inflicting a wound,[28] making a cleft in the rock, a hollow place in the cliff as an abode for doves.

Arise, therefore, beloved of Christ, *be ye like the dove that maketh her nest in the mouth of the hole in the highest place*; there, as a bird that has found a nest, do not cease to keep watch; there, like the turtledove, hide the offspring of your chaste love; there, apply your mouth to *draw waters with joy out of the Saviour's fountains*. For this, indeed, is the river rising from the midst of paradise which divided into four branches, and flowing into devout hearts, waters the whole earth and makes it fertile.

JESUS COVERED WITH BLOOD

31. Christ the Lord was crimsoned with His own blood, flowing in abundance: first with the sweat of the agony, then with the lashes and thorns, then with the nails, and finally with the spear-thrust. That He might become a *plenteous redemption* before the Lord, He wore a priestly robe of scarlet; His apparel was truly red, and His garments were *like theirs that tread in the wine press*. Like that of a true Joseph thrown into an abandoned cistern, His tunic was steeped as in the blood of a goat—that is, blood shed *in the likeness of sinful flesh*—and sent to the Father for identification and recognition.

"Recognize, therefore, O most merciful Father, the tunic of Your beloved Son Joseph whom the hatred of His brothers in the flesh has devoured, like a wild beast; whose garments it has trampled in rage, befouling the beautiful apparel with blood, leaving on it five ugly gashes. This indeed, O Lord, is the garment which Your innocent Son willingly abandoned into the hands of the evil woman of Egypt, that is, the Synagogue; for He preferred to be deprived of His clothing of flesh and to descend into the prison of death rather than seek a passing glory by yielding to the cries of an adulterous mob." Jesus, instead of *the joy set before Him, endured a cross, despising shame.*[29]

And do you, most merciful Lady of mine, behold this most sacred vestment of your beloved Son, artistically woven by the Holy Spirit from your most chaste body; and, together with Him, beg for mercy for us who take refuge in you, so that we may be found worthy *to flee from the wrath to come*.

JESUS LAID IN THE TOMB

32. With the permission of Pilate, a noble man named Joseph of Arimathea, assisted by Nicodemus, took down the body of Christ from the cross, embalmed it with spices, and wrapping it in a shroud,

---

[28] Inflicting a wound: The Vulgate, quoted here by St. Bonaventure, has "casso vulnere" which means "failing to wound." Our author seems to interpret "casso" as "quasso."

[29] The Confraternity text has "for the joy," meaning "in the expectation of the joy." St. Bonaventure seems to prefer another accepted meaning. Cf. Cornelius a Lapide, "Commentaria," loc. cit.

buried it with great reverence in a tomb recently cut in the rock for his own use in a garden nearby. After Christ was buried and soldiers were assigned to watch His tomb, the devout and holy women who had followed in His company when He was alive, wishing to perform the offices of piety now that He was dead, brought spices with which to complete the embalming of His most sacred body. Among them was Mary Magdalene.

Such intense fervor burned in her heart, such sweet pity inundated her, such strong bonds of love drew her, that womanly weakness was forgotten and neither the darkness of night nor the brutality of the persecutors could keep her from the tomb. Even the disciples had fled; yet she did not flee, but remained before the sepulcher, drenching the stone with her tears. Set afire by the divine flame, she burned with such a powerful desire, and suffered a wound of such impatient love, that nothing but tears had any taste for her. In all truth, she could have uttered these words of the prophet: "*My tears are my food day and night, as they say to me day after day, 'Where is your God?'*"

O my God, Jesus all-good! Unworthy though I am in nature and merits, grant that since I had not the privilege of being present in the body at these events, I may at least faithfully consider them in my mind, and feel toward You, my God, crucified and put to death for me, the very compassion Your innocent Mother and the penitent Magdalene experienced at the hour of Your passion.

III. ON THE MYSTERY OF THE GLORIFICATION

NINTH FRUIT: THE WONDER OF HIS RESURRECTION

JESUS, TRIUMPHANT IN DEATH

33. Now that the agony of the passion was over, and the bloody dragon and the savage lion thought they had obtained victory by murdering the Lamb, the power of divinity began to shine forth in His soul descending into hell. Through this power, our strong *Lion of the tribe of Juda*, rising against His fully armed foe, tore away its prey, broke down the gates of hell, and shackled the serpent. *Disarming the Principalities and Powers, He displayed them openly, leading them away in triumph.* Now Leviathan has been led about with a hook, his jaw pierced by Christ Himself. Thus Satan, who had no power over the Head he had assaulted, lost also any power he had seemed to have over the body. It was then that the true Samson destroyed by His death a whole army of enemies; then, that the immaculate Lamb delivered His prisoners *by the blood of* His *testament*, and *sent forth* His *prisoners out of the pit wherein is no water*; then, that the radiance of a new light long expected shone upon those *that dwelt in the region of the shadow of death.*

JESUS RISING IN GLORY

34. At dawn, on the third day of the Lord's holy repose in the tomb—at a point of time that is both first and last in the weekly cycle—Christ, the Power and Wisdom of God, having overcome the author of death, vanquished death itself, opened for us the way to eternity by rising from the dead through His divine might, and showed us *the path to life.*

Now, *there was a great earthquake; for an angel of the Lord came down from heaven.... His countenance was like lightning, and his raiment like snow.* Gentle did he appear to the devout, but awesome to the wicked, in that he terrified the cruel soldiers but comforted the timid women. It was to these women that the Lord showed Himself first: a favor they had earned by the greatness of their love. Next He was seen by Peter, then by the disciples on their way to Emmaus, then by all the apostles with the exception of Thomas. Later, He appeared to Thomas also, and invited him to touch His wounds; whereupon Thomas declared his faith: "*My Lord and my God!*" Christ appeared in this way to His disciples on many occasions *during forty days*, eating and drinking with them. He enlightened our faith with proofs, lifted up our hope with promises, so as finally to inflame our love with gifts from heaven.

JESUS, UTMOST BEAUTY

35. This beautiful flower *of the root of Jesse*, who had blossomed in the Incarnation and withered in the passion, now blossomed anew in the resurrection, so as to become our own crown of beauty. His most glorious body, subtile, agile, and immortal, is suffused with such radiant glory that He truly outshines the sun, forecasting how beautiful the human body will be at its own resurrection. Of this, indeed, the Saviour Himself has said: "*Then the just will shine forth like the sun in the kingdom of their Father*"—that is, in eternal beatitude. And if the just will shine forth like the sun, consider how brightly will then shine the glory of the very Sun of Justice! So bright, indeed, will be His refulgence that it is *fairer than the sun, and surpasses every constellation of the stars; compared to light,* His splendor *takes precedence,* and in all truth, may be called "matchless beauty."

Happy the eyes that have seen! As for you, happy will you be if there remain of your seed to see, both in mind and body, this Splendor, worthy of all desire.

JESUS, LORD OF THE EARTH

36. Jesus appeared to His disciples also in Galilee. There He declared to them that all power in heaven and earth had been given to Him by the Father. In virtue of this same power, He sent the disciples *into the whole world to preach the gospel to every creature.* He promised salvation to those who would believe their message, and threatened with reprobation those who would reject it. *The Lord worked with them and confirmed the preaching by the signs that followed,* giving them power over all creatures and all diseases *in the name of Jesus Christ.* For the whole world is to acknowledge that Jesus Christ, Son of the Father Almighty, as another Joseph and as a true Saviour, lives and reigns, not only over the land of Egypt, but indeed "everywhere in the eternal King's domain: for He has been called up from the prison of death and of the nether world to the heavenly King's throne. Shorn of the fleece of mortality, He has exchanged the clothing of flesh for the splendor of eternal life. Like a true Moses rescued from the deadly waters, He has defeated the power of Pharao." So lofty is His honor that at His name *every knee should bend of those in heaven, on earth, and under the earth.*

TENTH FRUIT: THE SUBLIMITY OF HIS ASCENSION

JESUS, LEADER OF THE HOST

37. Forty days after the Lord's resurrection—and there is a mysterious meaning in this fortieth day—the good Master, having shared a meal with His disciples, went up with them to Mount Olivet. There, *He lifted up His hands ... and was carried up into heaven, and before their eyes, ... a cloud took Him out of their sight,* and He disappeared. Thus He *ascended on high, and* has *led captivity captive*; and the gates of heaven now being open, He led the way

for those who were to follow Him, and introduced the exiles into the kingdom. He made them fellow citizens of the angels and *members of God's household*; compensating for the angels' fall, increasing His Father's honor, revealing Himself as a triumphant Victor, as the Lord of Hosts.

JESUS RISEN TO HEAVEN

38. While the angels sang and the saints exulted for joy, the God and Lord of angels and men rode *on the heights of the ancient heavens, borne on the wings of the wind.* With the wondrous ease of power, He soared aloft and came to rest at the right hand of the Father, *having become so much superior to the angels as He has inherited a more excellent name than they.* And there, at the same time, He appeared *before the face of God on our behalf—For it was fitting that we should have such a High Priest, holy, innocent, undefiled, set aside from sinners, and become higher than the heavens*, so that, seated at the right hand of Majesty, He might show His Father the scars of the glorious wounds He had suffered for our sake.

"May every tongue give thanks to You, O Lord our Father, for the ineffable gift of Your most generous love. Indeed, You have not spared even Your own Son, but have *delivered Him for us all* unto death so that we might have a great and faithful Advocate in heaven before Your face."

JESUS, GIVER OF THE SPIRIT

39. Seven weeks after the resurrection, on the fiftieth day, the disciples were *all together in one place with the women and Mary, the Mother of Jesus.—And suddenly there came a sound from heaven, as of a violent wind blowing.* There descended upon the group of *a hundred and twenty* people the likeness of tongues of fire, to give to the mouth the fire of speech, to the mind, that of light, and to the heart, that of love. *And they were all filled with the Holy Spirit and began to speak in foreign tongues, even as the Holy Spirit prompted them to speak*: for He taught them all truth, inflamed them with all love, and strengthened them in every virtue. Assisted by His grace, enlightened by His teaching, and strengthened by His might, the disciples, few and simple as they were, planted the Church in their blood throughout the world, with their fiery words, the perfection of their example, and their astonishing miracles. The Church, cleansed, enlightened, and perfected by the might of the same Holy Spirit, thus became lovable to her Spouse and His attendants for being so exceedingly beautiful and so admirably adorned with variety; but to Satan and his minions, she became as *awe-inspiring as bannered troops.*

JESUS, FORGIVER OF SINS

40. Assisted by the marvelous works of the Holy Spirit, this Church, richly varied yet so strictly one throughout the world, is presided over by the One Christ, High Priest and supreme Hierarch. By a wonderful organization similar to that of the heavenly city, He establishes the various churchly offices and functions through the distribution of the charismatic gifts. *He Himself gave some men as apostles, and some as prophets, others again as evangelists, and others as pastors and teachers, in order to perfect the saints for a work of ministry, for building up the body of Christ.*

Also, in parallel with the sevenfold graces of the Holy Spirit, He established, as seven remedies against sickness, the seven sacraments. Through them He both granted sanctifying grace and remitted sins, which can never be forgiven outside the faith and the fold of Holy Mother Church.

Since the cleansing of sins is through the fire of tribulation, and since God has exposed the Head of the Church to the full torrent of sufferings, even so He has permitted His body, that is, His Church, to suffer tribulations until the end of time for the sake of its own proving and purification. Thus, patriarchs and prophets, apostles and martyrs, confessors and virgins, and all who have ever been pleasing to God have remained faithful in the face of many trials. And so will remain all the chosen members of Christ until the day of judgment.

ELEVENTH FRUIT: THE EQUITY OF HIS JUDGMENT

JESUS, TRUTHFUL WITNESS

41. At the time of the judgment to come, when God is to weigh the secrets of hearts, fire will precede the arrival of the Judge; angels will be sent with trumpets to gather the elect from the four winds of heaven; all those who lie in their tombs will rise through the power of God's command, and will stand before His judgment seat. Then the things hidden in darkness will be brought to light, and the counsels of hearts will be made manifest, and the scrolls of men's consciences will be unrolled, and that scroll itself will be opened which is called the Book of Life. Thus, together and in a single flash, all the secrets of all men will be revealed to all with such clear certainty that, before the evidence of Truth testifying in the Person of Christ and corroborated by the testimony of every separate conscience, not a single path will be left open for denial or defense, for excuse or evasion, but every man will then receive according to his deeds. "Therefore, there is a compelling reason for us to be good: all our acts are in full sight of an all-seeing Judge."

JESUS, SEVERE JUDGE

42. When the sign of the omnipotent Son of God appears in the clouds, when *the powers of heaven will be shaken* and add their cosmic fires to the general conflagration of the earth, when all the just have been placed at the right hand of God and the wicked at His left, the Judge of the Universe will appear so wrathful to the reprobate that they will say *to the mountains and to the rocks, "Fall upon us and hide us from the face of Him who sits upon the throne, and from the wrath of the Lamb."*—He shall don justice for a breastplate and shall wear sure judgment for a helmet; He shall take invincible rectitude as a shield and whet His sudden anger for a sword, and the universe shall war with Him against the foolhardy; so that those who had fought with malice against the Maker of all shall then be condemned by all, by a just judgment of God.

"Then, the Judge in His wrath will appear on high; below, hell will gape as a fearful chaos; on the right side will be the accusing legions of sins, on the left, the countless host of demons; and so, for the trapped sinner, there is no escape. Certainly, to hide will be impossible, and to be seen, unbearable. And if *the just man scarcely will be saved, where will the impious and the sinner appear?*"

O Lord, … enter not into judgment with Your servant!

JESUS, GLORIOUS CONQUEROR

43. Having sentenced the reprobate to eternal fire, Almighty God will throw them, in the flesh and in the spirit—the enemies of Christ now become as bundles—to feed the voracity of everlasting flames; never to perish but always to burn and suffer. *And the smoke of their torments goes up forever and ever.*— Then *the beast and the false prophet … and those who accepted … its image*[30] shall be cast *into the pool of fire that burns with brimstone … —which was prepared for the devil and his angels.* And the just *shall go out and see the carcasses*—dead, indeed, not by the death of nature but by the death of penalty; then the just shall dip their hands in the blood of the sinners; then at last the triumphant Lamb shall make His enemies His footstool, while the wicked *go into the depths of the earth*, and are *delivered over to the sword*, and become *the prey of jackals*, meaning the demons who had seduced them through guile.

JESUS, RADIANT SPOUSE

44. Finally, when the whole face of the earth has been renewed, when *the light of the moon shall be as the light of the sun, and the light of the sun shall be sevenfold, as the light of seven days*, when *the holy city, Jerusalem, coming down out of heaven* as a bride adorned, prepared *for the marriage of the Lamb*, and clad with a double stole,[31] shall be led to the palace

---

[30] *and … image*: has not this construction in the Vulgate.

[31] Cf. Bonaventure, "Breviloquium," VII, 7:1.

where the heavenly court abides, and introduced into the holy and secret bridal chamber: then this holy city shall be united to the heavenly Lamb with a covenant so closely binding that bride and groom will become *one spirit*. Then Christ shall be clothed with all the beauty of the elect as if with a *long tunic* variously adorned, in which He shall shine as if covered with all manner of precious stones. Then the sweet wedding song shall rise, and throughout Jerusalem the people shall sing: Alleluia! Then the prudent and well-prepared virgins shall go in with the Spouse to *the marriage feast*, and, the door being closed, *shall sit in the beauty of peace, and in the tabernacle of confidence, and in wealthy rest.*

TWELFTH FRUIT: THE ETERNITY OF HIS KINGDOM

JESUS, KING AND PRINCE

45. How glorious and noble God's kingdom is, we must learn from the dignity of its King, since a king is not derived from a kingdom, but the kingdom from the king.[32] And He, indeed, is King who wears on *His garment and on His thigh a name written: King of kings and Lord of lords*; whose *power is an everlasting power that shall not be taken away*; whose kingdom shall never be destroyed; and whom nations and peoples and tongues shall serve throughout eternity. And He is truly *Peaceable*, upon whose countenance all heaven and earth desire to look.

Oh, how glorious is the kingdom of this lofty King where all the just share the reign with God! Its laws are truth, peace, love, life, and eternity. Its rulers are many, yet it is undivided; although shared by all, it is not lessened; the multitude causes no confusion in it, the inequality of ranks, no discord; no borders confine it in space, no commotion alters it, nor is its course measured by time.

JESUS, INSCRIBED SCROLL

46. To be perfect, a kingdom's glory demands not only supreme authority, but also enlightened wisdom, so that the state is not guided by whim but by the beams of eternal laws which safely radiate from Wisdom's beacon. And this very Wisdom is found in Jesus Christ, as in the Book of Life in which God the Father has *hidden all the treasures of wisdom and knowledge*. Therefore, the only-begotten Son of God, as the Uncreated Word, is the Book of Wisdom and the Light, replete with the eternal principles alive in the highest Maker's mind; as the Inspired Word, He dwells in the minds of the angels and the blessed; as the Incarnate Word, He dwells in spiritual minds which are still united with flesh. Thus, throughout the kingdom, *the manifold wisdom of God* shines forth from Him and in Him, as in a mirror containing the beauty of all ideas and lights, or as in a book in which all things are written according to God's deep secrets.

Oh, to find this book of which the origin is eternal; the essence, incorruptible; the science, life-giving; the writing, indelible; the study, desirable; the teaching, easy; the knowledge, sweet; the depth, inscrutable; the words, ineffable; yet all this in a single Word! Truly, whoever finds this Book shall *find life, shall have salvation from the Lord.*

JESUS, FONT OF LIGHT

47. In this eternal kingdom, *every good gift and every perfect gift* comes down in plenty and abundance *from the Father of Lights*, through Jesus Christ who is the super-essential beam: for He *who is One, can do all things, and renews everything* while Himself perduring. He is *an aura of the might of God and a pure effusion of the glory of the Almighty; therefore nought that is sullied enters into* this Font of Light.

All you souls devoted to God, run with intense desire to this Fountain of Life and Light, and cry out to Him with all the power of your hearts: "O inaccessible Beauty of God most high, purest Clarity of the Eternal Light, Life imparting life to every life,

---

[32] This is an application of the obsolete theory of kingship by divine right.

Light imparting light to every light, keeping in eternal brilliance a thousand times a thousand lamps that brightly shine ever since the primeval dawn! O eternal and inaccessible, clear and sweet Stream from the Fountain invisible to all mortal eyes: Your depth knows no bottom, Your width knows no shore, Your vastness no bounds, Your clearness no taint!"

From this Fountain comes forth the stream of *the oil of gladness…—whose runlets gladden the city of God*, and the powerful and fiery torrent of the pleasure of God, filling with joyful inebriation the celestial guests who forever sing their hymns of praise. Anoint us with this sacred oil; quench with the longed-for waters of this torrent the thirst of our burning hearts, so that, *amid loud cries of joy and thanksgiving*, we may sing to You a canticle of praise and learn by experience that *with You is the Fountain of life, and in Your Light we see light.*

JESUS, DESIRED END

48. It is a fact that all desires tend to happiness, which is "a perfect state consisting in the simultaneous presence of all goods." No one reaches this state except through a final union with Him who is the foundation and origin of goods both natural and supernatural, both bodily and spiritual, both temporal and eternal. He it is who says of Himself: "*I am the Alpha and the Omega, the Beginning and the End!*" As all things are brought forth through the Word eternally uttered, so through the Word made flesh all things are restored, impelled, and achieved. Hence, He is truly and properly called Jesus: *for there is no other name under heaven given to men by which we must be saved.*

By believing, hoping, loving, with my whole heart, and with my whole soul, and with my whole mind, and with my whole strength, may I be carried to You, O beloved Jesus, Goal of all: for You alone are all-sufficient, You alone do save, You alone are good and delightful to those who seek You and *love Your name*. "For You, O my good Jesus, are the Redeemer of the lost, the Saviour of the redeemed, the hope of exiles, the strength of laborers, the sweet consolation of anguished minds, the crown and imperial canopy of the triumphant, the only reward and joy of all the citizens of heaven, the glorious offspring of the highest God, the sublime fruit of the virginal womb, the abundant fountain of all graces, *of whose fullness we have all received.*"

PRAYER FOR THE SEVEN GIFTS OF THE HOLY SPIRIT

49. We pray the Father most kind through You, His only-begotten Son, who for us became Man and were crucified and glorified, that He send us, out of the abundance of His wealth, the Spirit of sevenfold grace that rested upon You in all fullness: the gift of WISDOM, that we may taste in its life-giving flavor the fruit of the Tree of Life which You truly are; the gift of UNDERSTANDING, through which the vision of our mind is clarified; the gift of COUNSEL, that we may follow in Your footsteps and proceed along the paths of righteousness; the gift of FORTITUDE, that we may meet the violence of our enemies' assaults; the gift of KNOWLEDGE, that we may be filled with the light of Your sacred teaching to distinguish good from evil; the gift of PIETY, that our hearts may be filled with kindness; the gift of FEAR, that we may draw away from all evil and be kept in peace by the awesome might of Your majesty. For You have willed that we ask for these things in the holy prayer which You taught us: so now we beg them of You, in the name of Your cross, in praise of Your most holy name. To You, and to the Father, and to the Holy Spirit, be all glory and honor and thanksgiving, all splendor and power, forever and ever! Amen.

The Mystical Vine Treatise on the Passion of the Lord

Vitis Mystica seu Tractatus de Passione Domini

A Devout Meditation

Prologue

I AM THE TRUE VINE.... O Jesus, come! O kindly Vine, Tree of Life standing in the midst of the garden! O Lord Jesus Christ, whose leaves are medicine and whose fruit is eternal life! O You who are blessed as both the Flower and the Fruit of the holy parentstem, the most chaste Virgin Mother; You beside whom no one is wise since You are the Wisdom of the eternal Father! Deign to strengthen with *the bread of understanding* and the *water of learning* my soul, feeble and parched, so that, as You open, O Key of David, hidden truths may be revealed to me; and as You shine, O *True Light*, obscure things may become luminous; and as You manifest Yourself, and make Yourself known through me, both I who speak and all who listen may attain eternal life. Amen.

Chapter I—On the Properties of the Vine

1. "*I am the True Vine....*" With the help of our Lord Jesus Christ Himself, let us consider some of the properties of the earthly vine, whereby we may discover those of the Vine from heaven. Let us study, not only its own natural properties, but also the methods of its cultivation.

2. First, we observe that a vine is planted as a cutting, not as a seed; it is transferred to the soil from another vine. This we may see as a symbol of the conception of Jesus: for the Vine first to be born of a Vine is God begotten of God, the Son begotten of the Father, coeternal and consubstantial with Him from whom He proceeds. But in order to produce more fruit, this Vine was planted in the soil: it was conceived in the Virgin Mary's womb, becoming what it had not been, yet remaining what it was.

O blessed soil, producing the Blessing of all nations! Truly blessed, indeed, since through God's loving-kindness it brought forth such blessed Fruit! This is the soil of which it is written: *There was no man to till the soil; but ... a river rose in Eden, watering the garden.* No human labor prepared this soil for the conception of God's Son: the garden was irrigated with the water of the Holy Spirit. It is written: "*The Holy Spirit shall come upon thee and the power of the Most High shall overshadow thee.*" It is also written of this soil: *Let the earth be opened and bud forth a Saviour.* This earth, that is, the blessed Virgin Mary, opened through faith, for she believed and heeded the words of the angel. And this soil budded forth the saving Vine, our Saviour, "who bestows the reward of eternal life."

When our Vine had thus appeared, some of the practices of viticulture were applied to Him.

Chapter II—On the Pruning of the Vine

1. A fruit-bearing vine is pruned. This may be understood in a physical or a figurative sense. Our Lord Jesus Christ was in fact circumcised, but not because He was subject to the law of circumcision. It was in order that the pain of our sufferings might be lightened through the pain of Him who suffered, not for His own sake, but for ours; who was wounded, not on His own account, but in order to heal our wounds.

2. We may also understand the pruning of this Vine, our most loving Jesus, in a different sense by saying that those things which He could have had in this life, but did not have, were cut away from Him. Let us accept this as being the intent of the apostle's words: *Who though He was by nature God ... emptied Himself, taking the nature of a slave.* This emptying is pruning, in a way; for as the vine, when pruned, is lessened, so the True Vine, the Lord Jesus Christ, in His Incarnation was made *less than the angels;* humbled, in fact, more deeply than any man.

3. How? Glory was cut away from Him with the knife of shame, power with the knife of abjection, pleasure with the knife of pain, wealth with the knife of poverty. And now, behold how much was cut away. He to whom all heaven renders glory, who alone is Glory itself, casting off, as it were, this glory, takes on the garment of a slave, endures ignominy, and is covered with shame, in order to redeem us from shame and restore our pristine glory. All things in hell, on earth, and in high heaven are subject to His all-powerful will; yet He is made so lowly as to be considered *the most abject of men*. He suffers hunger and thirst, heat, cold, and weakness; also, the final torments of death itself. He *dwells in light inaccessible;* the holy *angels desire to look* upon Him; His mere fragrance inebriates the minds of the saints, so that they run to Him with all their might, forgetting this world and forgetting their own selves; yet He is subjected to suffering until His words, uttered in days of old through the prophet, are clearly known to be fulfilled: "*O all ye that pass by the way, attend, and see if there be any sorrow like to My sorrow!*"

In Him are hidden all the treasures of wisdom and knowledge, He is rich in all things, and, in Himself, lacks nothing; yet He becomes poor to the extent of being found poorer, in His own words, than the foxes of the earth and the birds of the air. For He says: "*The foxes have dens and the birds of the air have nests; but the Son of Man has nowhere to lay His head.*" Born poor, He lived poorer, and died on the cross poorest of all. As a baby, He was fed with virginal milk, and was wrapped in plain swaddling clothes; in adult life, He often lacked food, even though He had clothing; in death, we find Him naked and thirsting—unless it can be said that *wine ... mixed with gall* quenched His thirst.

4. Finally, all His friends and relatives were cut from Him with the knife of fear, so that there was none to comfort Him among all those who were dear to Him. He has trodden the wine press alone: of the Gentiles, there was not a man with Him. His heart breaking under the insults. He looked around for sympathy, but there was none; for comforters, and He found none. Behold, then, how much our Vine, the most loving Jesus, has been cut. What other vine was ever pruned so heavily? But the consoling aspect of this cutting is the abundance of fruit yielded by the great, the matchless sacrifice.

Chapter III—On the Digging around the Vine

1. A vine is also dug around. Such digging means, in this case, an enemy stratagem, since a malicious attempt to entrap someone is like digging a pit for him. *They have dug a pit before me*, the prophet complains. But no ruse could be concealed from the One who is *full of eyes before and behind*, and who sees past and future as if they were present.

Let us illustrate this by a particular instance. According to the Gospel, the Pharisees brought before Jesus a woman caught in adultery, and said to Him: "*In the Law, Moses commanded us to stone such persons. What, therefore, dost Thou say?*" Behold the pits set before the true Vine; how they were dug around this blessed Vine of ours, the most loving Lord Jesus, by the evil gardeners whose purpose was not to help it grow, but to make it wither. Their wicked plan, however, had the opposite result: the Vine, dug around, grew large and produced for us the wine of mercy.

2. It would take much too long to describe all the pits dug by these evil gardeners. They were constantly trying to find fault with Christ's every word and deed. As soon as they realized, however, that they were not

harming Him, but on the contrary were falling into their own pits, they gave up digging around the Vine, and worked instead at digging into the Vine, hoping that it would thus wither away permanently like an ordinary growth. And so they dug and bored, not only His hands, but also His feet and His side; they transfixed with the spear of fury the core of His most sacred heart, which had already been opened with the spear of love.

"*Thou hast wounded My heart, My sister, My bride; thou hast wounded My heart.*" Your bride, Your sister, Your friend, has wounded Your heart, O most loving Jesus! Why did it have to be wounded again by Your enemies? And you, enemies, what are you doing? Since the heart of the most sweet Jesus is already wounded, why inflict upon it a second wound? Do you not know that a single wound is enough to cause a heart to die and to lose its capacity to suffer? Wounded, the heart of my sweet Lord Jesus died: the wound of love, the death of love, held within its power the heart of Jesus the Spouse. What other death could enter there? For *love is strong as death*; even stronger. The first death—death through love for the multitude of dead souls—cannot be expelled from the shelter of the heart, for it has been gained through an inviolable wound. When two men contend whose strength is equal, and one is inside the house while the other is outside, who would doubt that the one inside will win? How strong must that love be that possesses the mansion of the heart, and kills by the very wound of desire; which is the case not only of the Lord Jesus but also of His followers.

So, the heart of Jesus had been wounded to death for a long time: *For Your sake we are being slain all the day; we are looked upon as sheep to be slaughtered.* Then physical death was added—victorious for a time, only to be vanquished for eternity.

3. Since we have already entered the heart of the most sweet Lord Jesus, and since it is *good for us to be here*, let us not be easily expelled from it: for *they that depart from Thee shall be written in the earth.* And what of those who come close to You? Let us come close to You, says King Solomon, and *we will be glad and rejoice*, remembering Your heart. How good and pleasant it is to dwell in this heart, O dearest Jesus! this heart which is the rich treasure we have found in the plowed-up field of Your body. Who would reject such a pearl? Should I not rather give up all my other jewels, exchange all my former thoughts and affections, for this treasure? I will cast my troubles upon the heart of the good Jesus, and that heart will never fail me.

4. To this Temple, to this Holy of Holies, to this Ark of the Covenant, I will come to adore and to praise the Lord's name, saying with David: "I have found my heart that I may pray this prayer to Thee." But the heart I have found is the heart of my King and Lord, of my Brother and Friend, the most loving Jesus; then shall I not pray? Yes, I will pray, for I say without hesitation that His heart is also mine. And since Christ is my Head, how could that which belongs to my Head not also belong to me? As the eyes of my bodily head are truly my own, so also is the heart of my spiritual Head. Oh, what a blessed lot is mine to have one heart with Jesus! But no marvel, this, since also *the multitude of the believers were of one heart.*

Having found this heart, both Yours and mine, O most sweet Jesus, I will pray to You, my God. Admit my prayer into Your holy court of audience—yes, draw my whole being within Your heart. True, the crookedness of my sins keeps me from entering. But this heart is widened and broadened with a love beyond understanding, and You who alone are, can *make him clean that is conceived of unclean seed.* Therefore, O Most Beautiful of all beings, *thoroughly wash me from my guilt and of my sin cleanse me*; that, so purified, I may come to You, Most Pure, and be made worthy of living in Your heart *all the days of my life*, both knowing and doing Your will.

5. Your side was pierced so that an entrance might be opened there for us; Your heart was wounded so that, free from all worldly tribulations, we might live in that Vine; but Your heart was also wounded in order that, through the visible wound, we might see the invisible wound of love. For one who ardently loves is wounded by love. How could Christ better show us this ardor than by permitting not only His body but His very heart to be pierced with a lance?

The wound of the flesh reveals the wound of the spirit. This is well suggested in the Canticle quoted above, where it is said twice: *Thou hast wounded....* The sister and bride is the cause of both these wounds, as if the Spouse were clearly saying: "Because you have wounded Me with the zeal of your love, I have also been wounded with the soldier's spear." Who, indeed, would let his heart be wounded for the sake of one beloved if he had not first received from her the wound of love? That is why the Spouse says: "*Thou hast wounded My heart, My sister, My bride: thou hast wounded My heart.*"

But why "sister and bride"? Could not the Lover's affection be sufficiently evinced by mentioning either sister or bride? Again, why bride and not wife? Does not the Church itself, does not every faithful soul, day after day and without respite, give birth to the progeny of good works unto Christ the Spouse? Let me attempt to answer this question briefly.

A bride is often more ardently loved while the union is new than later, when love has settled down with the passing of time. Thus, our Spouse, in order to make us understand the intensity of His love, which does not decrease with time, calls His beloved a bride, because His love is always new.

6. But brides are also the object of physical love. In order to eliminate all taint of carnality from our idea of our Spouse's love, the bride is called also a sister; for sisters are never the object of carnal love. That is why Solomon says: "*Thou hast wounded My heart, My sister, My bride,*" as if saying: "Because I love you as intensely as I would a bride, and as chastely as I would a sister, My heart is wounded on your behalf."

Who could fail to love the heart that bears such a wound? Who could fail to return the love of such a Lover? Who would not embrace such chastity? The bride, wounded with this mutual love, assuredly loves the wounded heart when she cries out: "*I am wounded with love.*" She returns the love of the Spouse when she says: "Tell my Beloved that I am faint with love."

As for us who are still dwelling in the flesh, let us return His love as fully as we can; let us embrace our wounded Christ whose hands and feet and side and heart were pierced by the wicked vine-tenders; let us pray that He may deign to tie our hearts, now so wild and impenitent, with the bond of love, and wound them with love's spear. Amen.

Chapter IV—On the Tying of the Vine

1. A vine is tied. Who could fail to see the bonds of our Vine? Let us look at them. The first bond is seen to be obedience. He obeyed the Father *to death, even to death on a cross*. He obeyed both His Mother and Joseph, according to these words: *And He ... came to Nazareth, and was subject to them*. He also obeyed the judges of the world by paying the didrachma.

The second bond was the Virgin's womb: "for Him whom the heavens cannot contain, thou hast carried within thy womb." The third bond was the manger, according to these words: "The Infant wailed as He was placed within a narrow manger." The fourth bond is to be seen in the ropes with which He was tied at the time of His arrest. *They ... set hands on Jesus and took Him.*

O King of kings and Lord of lords, what do bonds have to do with You? The vine is tied to keep the branches off the ground and thus prevent the loss or spoiling of the fruit. But Your fruit is incorruptible—why should You be bound? King Alexander answered well when, wounded by a barbed arrow, he was asked to let himself be bound while it was being pulled out, since the slightest movement might have caused his death. "It is not proper that a king be bound," he said. "Let a king's power always be free and undiminished."

O God of gods, what an offense against Your freedom and Your power! You to be bound with so many ropes who alone are free! You to be bound who alone have the power to bind and to release! But it was because of Your mercy that You submitted: it was in order that we might be freed from our miseries. Oh, the cruelty of the ropes with which those most cruel men tied the Lamb most mild! O Lord Jesus, I see You with the eyes of my mind—the only way now possible to me—tied with the rough rope, dragged like a bandit to the high priest's tribunal and then to Pilate. I see, and I am filled with horror and bewilderment. I would faint at the sight if I did not know with certainty that Your heart was first secured with the bonds of love, whose gentle might prompted You to accept the physical bond. O sweet Jesus, praised be Your bonds which so powerfully break our own.

2. The fifth bond was the rope by which Jesus was tied to the scourging post; although the very lashes of the scourge that were repeatedly wrapped around His body could also properly be called bonds. Cruel, harsh, and unjust as they were, I love the thongs of those infamous whips to which it was given to touch Your most holy body and to become steeped in Your most pure blood. O sweet Jesus, if Your blood ran so freely in the scourging that, according to legend, the post bespattered with it retains to this day some marks of red, how much more of Your blood must have soaked the scourges that actually cut into Your flesh! Behold how well the tying of a vine upon a stake can be applied to this binding. What truer stake could there be than that to which the Lord was tied? For as the vine is bound to a stake, so was Christ bound to the post.

3. The sixth bond was the crown of thorns that so cruelly pressed the beloved head of Christ, and left upon it the traces of its many spikes, drawing from every wound a trickle of blood that ran down, we may suppose, upon His sacred face where the spittle of the Jews had hardly dried. Oh, how cruel this bond, how dishonoring the pain brought about by the mock emblem of honor!

Who forced upon You this bitter bond of shame, O *King of glory*, O good Jesus, Crown of all who trust in You, follow You, fight for You, win through You, dwell in You? Behold, shame covers Your head and Your beloved face. From an *unbelieving and perverse generation* comes a mockery of honor in the crown, but also the reality of pain, in the piercing thorns. Shame and pain are vying in You, and which makes You suffer more I do not know: the crown humiliates You, while the thorns pierce Your head.

Daughters of Jerusalem, come forth and look upon King Solomon in the crown with which His mother has crowned Him on the day of His marriage, *on the day of the joy of His heart.* Let every soul who calls herself a daughter of Sion, that is, of the Church, give up all worldly care and all vain thought. Through contemplation, let her look upon *King Solomon*—which signifies Jesus Christ, who *is our Peace*; who puts an end to warfare and restores friendship between God and man.

Behold Him, O faithful soul, *in the crown with which His mother*—to wit, the Synagogue, or Jewish people—*has crowned Him.* O cruel mother, what crime did your good Son commit that you should enclose Him within thorny bonds? He is the One *who secures justice for the oppressed* of your race, who *raises up those that were bowed down* ... who sustains *the fatherless and the widow.* Does such a one have to be bound? Is this the gift you have brought to Him? Are these your wedding presents? *The day of His marriage* is the first day, that day of indignity and blasphemy, of tribulation and misery, of blows and pain, of bonds and death. Such is this wedding day, O faithful soul, and such is the dowry by which your Spouse, *who is fairer in beauty ... than the sons of men*, has betrothed you. He Himself on this day *comes forth like the groom*, crowned, not with gold and jewels, but with thorns. Nor was purple lacking in His clothing of derision, for *they put on Him a scarlet cloak*; although He Himself empurpled His bodily garments in a much nobler fashion, by shedding His most holy blood. Scarlet cloth is not dyed more than twice. He purpled His body, not twice, but with a threefold torrent of blood.

O bride, look upon your Spouse turned scarlet by the bloody sweat, by the scourging, by the crucifixion! Lift up the eyes of your spirit and see whether or not this is the tunic of your Spouse! See, a wild beast, a rabid dog—the Judean mob—devours Him; a wild beast condemns your Son, your Brother, your Spouse! Who would not be filled with sorrow at the sight? Who could keep back sobs and tears? As it is a devout act to rejoice for Jesus, so it is devout to weep for Him.

4. The seventh bond, the one by which Jesus was attached to the cross, was made of iron. This bond was much stronger and much crueler than the others, for not only did iron tear apart the joints of His sacred

hands and feet, but it also separated this all-loving soul from its dwelling place, His most pure body.

Now, *daughters of Jerusalem, come forth and look* upon our Peacemaker fighting for our freedom, and falling in the battle. Behold the Author of our lives passing for our sake through the doors of death, in order to call us back to the path of life. Watch as the excruciating bonds, the iron spikes, cruelly penetrate the hands and feet that had always been intent on our salvation, and always had been the doers *of saving deeds on earth*. Behold the wood of the cross cutting into our Bread, the Bread most pure, the Bread having within it all delight, *the Bread of angels—which comes down from heaven* in order that Christ might give Himself to us as food; in order that our souls, which are under the need of laboring without pause, might be restored by Him and by no other fare; in order that He might become flesh in us, not for the sake of transforming Himself into our flesh but to transform us into His spirit. Beloved soul, behold how He was bound, how *He was reckoned among the wicked*, He, our Spouse, who is Freedom and Goodness itself! Our Life dies, not because He need die, but because of our needs. Pour out a torrent of tears for Him who is dying in such bonds, since He first wept for us. Stand close to Him as He hangs, *be still and see* to what a bitter, shameful death He is condemned. He is still bearing His pain, looking for one to grieve with Him, to comfort Him; to wipe away the streams of blood, close His eyes, pull out the nails that hold Him fast; to lower Him from the cross with a clean cloth—not of linen but of the heart—and, sharing the tears of the weeping holy women, to bring Him to the tomb.

5. Following the advice of the blessed apostle Paul, *let us therefore go forth* to our Spouse, Jesus, bountiful and sovereign Goodness, *outside of the camp*, that is, outside of the concupiscence of this world; *bearing* with Him the *reproach* of the cross and the harshness of the bonds. For, in the words of Bernard, "it is not fitting that, under a crucified Head, there should be a delicate member"; nor does a member seem to belong to the same body as the head if it has not suffered with the head.

Let us be bound with the bonds of the passion of the good and most loving Jesus, so that we may also share with Him the bonds of love. For, made fast by these latter, He was drawn down from heaven to earth in order to suffer the former. Conversely, we who desire to be drawn from earth into heaven, must bind ourselves to our Head with the bonds of the passion, through which we will attain the bonds of love and thus become one with Him.

Chapter V—On the Likeness between Christ and the Vine, and First as Regards His Body

1. Now that we have considered some of the external aspects of vine cultivation, let us examine the vine in itself. By comparing it to our true Vine, the Lord Jesus Christ, we are able to behold Him more accurately and closely.

The whole trunk of the vine is gnarled, much more so than that of any other tree or shrub. It seems almost completely useless—of no value, and suited to no purpose. What does this signify? The body of the earthly vine should be a symbol of the Vine which is our Lord Jesus Christ—but how can that be when the one is so ugly and the Other so beautiful? It is written of Him: *"Fairer in beauty are You than the sons of men."* But listen now to Isaias: *There is no beauty in Him nor comeliness: and we have seen Him and there was no sightliness, that we should be desirous of Him: despised and the most abject of men, a Man of sorrows and acquainted with infirmity: and His look was as it were hidden and despised. Whereupon we esteemed Him not ... and we have thought Him as it were a leper, and as one struck by God and afflicted.* This is how the prophet describes Him.

2. But let us proceed to the effects of the passion. We do not apply the term "passion" to the one day only on which He died, but to the whole extent of His life; for the entire life of Christ was an example and a martyrdom. Though we set forth in a few words, let us ponder at length in our thoughts, His severe fastings, His long vigils, His frequent prayers, His

assiduous labors in the sweat of His brow, His untiring efforts as He went about the towns and villages, teaching, curing the sick. How often did He suffer hunger and thirst, He the *Bread of life*, He the *fountain of water springing up unto life everlasting!* Let us remember the forty-day fast, after which *He was hungry;* let us run to Him as He returns from the wilderness to the company of men; let us behold His beloved face!

3. Finally, let us consider the agony of the last day[33]: then we shall, of necessity, become aware of what disfigured His body. Let us first see Him in the place where, in His own words, His soul became *sad, even unto death*, as *He began to feel dread and to be exceedingly troubled*. While He lay there, agonizing and almost lifeless, a sweat of blood covered His limbs so abundantly that, instead of merely trickling, it ran down upon the ground. As we witness the further events of this dreadful night, we see Him seized, bound, dragged away, shoved around, beaten, spit upon, hit in the body and slapped in the face; we see Him crowned with thorns, clothed in a scarlet cloak, derided by mock adoration and genuflections, struck with a reed, ridiculed in a white vestment, torn with a sharp scourge, burdened with His own cross—for He was made to carry the cross that was to carry Him. This is the Jesus you are to behold! No room in Him for delight, no fairness in His face. Who in truth would look for any trace of beauty in this martyred body?

4. But let us now come to the final events. Our most loving Lord Jesus Christ is stripped of His clothes. Why? So that you may be able to see the ravages done to His most pure body. Therefore is this supremely good and sovereign Jesus despoiled. Alas, the Lord is stripped, He who was King before time began, *in splendor robed ... and girt about with strength;* He to whom we sing: *You are clothed with majesty and glory, robed in light as with a cloak*. He is *made a spectacle* and a shame *to the world ... and to men, as a portent ... to many*, and *a laughingstock among the peoples:* He, our Head, our Joy, our Honor, Jesus All-good! But why linger? He is lifted up on the cross, His hands and feet are pierced, His blood, what is left of it, is drained. Our Mediator hangs broken in the Father's sight *to turn back His destructive wrath*. And though His whole body is shattered, His mind does not waver, but stands firm in its loving resolve.

O tender Jesus, in what state do I behold You! O sweet, loving, all-giving Jesus, only Healer of our ancient wounds, who delivered You up to such a bitter death? Who forced You to bear these sufferings so intensely cruel and degrading? O most sweet Vine, bountiful Jesus! This is the fruit that was borne by the vineyard You have brought out of Egypt. Patiently, until this day of Your wedding, You had expected *that it should bring forth grapes*, but it brought forth thorns instead. For it has crowned You with thorns and with thorns hemmed You in. Oh, how bitter now and estranged, this vine that once belonged to You! For it denied You, proclaiming loudly: "*We have no king but Caesar*!"

5. After casting You out of the vineyard, that is, the city or society of men, these sacrilegious vine tenders killed You. And not with one blow: they put You to the slow torture of the cross and of the countless wounds made by the scourges and the nails.

O tender Jesus, how many are those who strike You! You are struck by Your Father, *who has not spared even His own Son*, but has delivered You for us all; You strike Yourself, for You have delivered up to death Your life, which none can take from You but Yourself; Your disciple strikes You by his treason and his deceitful kiss; the Jews strike You with blows on the body and face, and the Gentiles with scourges and nails! Behold how many times You have been struck and humiliated; how many were those who struck You!

And how many, also, are those who deliver You up! You are offered up by Your own Father, who has delivered You for us all; You offer Yourself up, as one of Your servants says in an outburst of gratitude: He *loved us and delivered Himself up for us*. O wonderful commerce! The Lord gives Himself up for the servant, God for man, the Creator for His creature, the Innocent for the sinner! For You have

---

[33] The "day" of the ancients begins at sundown.

surrendered Yourself into the hands of the betrayer, the false disciple, Judas; the betrayer sold You to the Jews; the Jews, in turn, wretched betrayers also, delivered You up to the Gentiles, to be mocked and spit upon, to be scourged and crucified. You told and foretold these things, and they came to pass. When all had been fulfilled, behold, You were crucified and *reckoned among the wicked*. Wounding You was not enough for them: they had to add *to the pain of Him* they had wounded, by giving You wine mixed with myrrh and gall to drink in Your thirst.

6. *I grieve for Thee*, my King, Lord and Master, Father and Brother, most loving Jesus; *amiable to me above the love of women*; whose *arrow ... never turned back*. For *Your arrows are sharp*—that is, Your teachings are strong; Your *word ... is living and efficient and keener than any two-edged sword, and extending even to the division of soul and spirit*; and Your shield did not retreat from battle, for You have surrounded us with the shield of benignity and of grace. The spear of Your prayer has not been turned away from us; for if You prayed for the offenders that they might not perish, how much more do You pray for Your friends!

You are stronger than a lion: You, *the Lion of the tribe of Juda*, who have overcome the lion that *goes about seeking someone to devour*. You are swifter than the eagle; for like a giant You have joyfully run Your course to the fulfillment of Your Incarnation until, as an eagle inciting its nestlings forth. You spread the wings of Your arms upon the cross. Hovering over us, You have received us and borne us on Your pinions; in Your strength, You have guided us to Your holy dwelling, to the mansion of Your intimacy and Your light. There, You have prepared a feast for Your neighbors and friends, causing the heavenly spirits to rejoice over a repentant sinner, as over the sheep and the drachma that were lost and found. Yet, in spite of Your perfection and Your majesty, You are condemned to a most shameful death; and after commending Your spirit into the hands of Your Father and inclining Your head, You do in verity yield up Your life.

7. Come, I pray, and share my sorrow, all of you who desire to rejoice in the Lord. Behold how your Strong One is broken, your Desirable One disfigured; behold your Peaceful One dying in battle. Where are now the cheeks flushed with life, the skin fair as snow? Where in this ravaged body will you find any beauty? Behold, they have passed away, the days of our Day, of Jesus most kind, the only Day without darkness. His bones have been parched like firewood, His heart cut down and dried like grass; He has been lifted up and cast down to the depths. Yet, throughout this external disgrace, He has kept all His inner beauty and honor.

Do not, then, despair for Him in His affliction. Those who are led only by appearances saw on the cross Him who is *fairer in beauty than the sons of men* deprived of beauty or human sightliness. They saw a disfigured face and a distorted body. Yet from this disfigurement of our Saviour flowed the price of our grace. We have seen, at least in part, the dark and outward ugliness of the body of our most loving Jesus. But who shall tell of the inner beauty of Him in whom *dwells all the fullness of the Godhead?* Let us, too, be deformed outwardly in our bodies, together with Jesus deformed, that we may be reformed internally, to companion Jesus most fair. Let us, in our own body, conform to the body of our Vine, so that *the body of our lowliness* may be reformed through conformity *to the body of His glory*.

Chapter VI—On the Second Likeness, That Is, the Leaves of the Vine: and First, in a General Way

1. The leaves of the vine stand out among those of most other trees. What else should these leaves be taken to represent but the words of our true Vine, Jesus most kind? As the Vine is exceptional by its leaves, so is Jesus by His words. And since the shade of vine leaves is generally more agreeable when the vine itself is supported by a wooden structure and thus spread out, let us see how our true Vine was also lifted up and stretched out. Let us consider, too, the foliage of sweet words He thus gave forth for our sheltering.

2. The Lord Jesus in person bears witness to His elevation, when He says of Himself: "*And I, if I be lifted up from the earth, will draw all things to Myself.*" There is no doubt that by this lifting up is meant the crucifixion. See how clearly the woodwork of the trellis upon which a vine is often spread symbolizes the cross. A trellis is a latticed structure, made of crossed pieces. It is upon this structure that the vine is spread out. What image could be closer? The beams of the gibbet are crossed; our Vine, the good Jesus, is lifted up on it; His arms and His whole body are forcibly stretched out—with such distorting violence have they been extended that all the joints of His frame can be counted. For the prophet says, "*They have dug My hands and feet, they have numbered all My bones*"; as if saying: They have stretched Me so much to the right and to the left and up and down that My body is as taut as the skin of a drum, and that all My bones could be easily counted.

3. *Look upon the face of your Anointed*, O Christian soul, and let your tearful eyes behold His torments; lift up your grieving heart to see the manifold afflictions He found while He was seeking you. Open your eyes wide upon the face of your Anointed; listen with eager ears to any word He may speak while in such pain. And whatever you hear, store as a most precious treasure in the secret vault of your heart. See, He is laid upon a cruel bed, the deathbed of the cross. Carefully preserve the last words of your Spouse if you wish to *earn an incorruptible inheritance, undefiled and unfading.* And since He did not utter many words in dying, the bride who has willingly chosen Christ will easily retain them.

Chapter VII—On the Leaves of the Vine in a Particular Way, and on the First Word of Christ on the Cross

1. Seven words, like seven leaves, ever green, came forth from our Vine aloft on the cross. Your Spouse has become a Harp, the wood of the cross being the frame and His body, extended on the wood, representing the chords. And these are the seven words.

2. First, while He was being nailed to the cross, the most loving Jesus said: "*Father, forgive them, for they do not know what they are doing.*" O verdant leaf! O word most worthy of the supreme Father's Word! The good Teacher follows His own teaching: He prays, not only for His friends, but also for those who persecute and calumniate Him. Hide this leaf within the treasury of your heart, so that whenever enemies assail you, you may recall the abounding sweetness of the good Jesus and always use this word as a shield against their insults. Your Spouse prays for those who are killing Him: can you not pray for those who are merely speaking evil of you?

3. But let us examine this prayer more closely. "Father," He says. Why is He using the word "Father"? When children affectionately ask something of their father, they are in the habit of calling him by this name to remind him, as it were, of his natural paternal love, and thus obtain more easily what they seek. Jesus also, *gracious and merciful, slow to anger and of great kindness, … and compassionate toward all*, while knowing full well that His Father always heard Him, resorted to this name of love so as to show us how sincerely we should pray for our enemies. It would seem that He was saying: In the name of the fatherly love by which We are One, I beg You on their behalf to hear Me, and pardon My murderers; to accept the love of Your Son, and forgive His enemies.

Chapter VIII—On the Second Leaf of the Vine, or the Second Word of Christ on the Cross

1. The second leaf of our Vine, and the second chord of our Harp, is the word that our Lord addressed to the thief who acknowledged Him and sought to be with Him. "*Amen,*" He said, "*I say to thee, this day thou shalt be with Me in paradise.*" What power in this leaf! How sweetly does this chord resound! How quickly has an enemy been changed

into a friend, a stranger into a member of the household, an alien into a close relative, a malefactor into a confessor! How great is this robber's confidence! He knows that everything in him is malice and nothing good, that he is a transgressor of the law, a ravisher of both the goods and the life of his neighbor. Now, in His last hour, on the threshold of death, despairing of this present life, he yet dares to seek reassurance in the hope of that future life which he has forfeited time and again, and has never deserved. Who could despair when this thief still hopes?

2. And so the Spouse listened to the soul, no longer a criminal's but a confessor's, now fully His. And as the prayer of this soul was acceptable, He comforted it, saying: *"Amen, I say to thee, this day thou shalt be with Me in paradise."* "To thee," that is, to the one who confessed Me on the cross of torture. "Thou shalt be with Me" in a paradise of delights: not merely "Thou shalt be in paradise," or "with the angels," but "thou shalt be *with Me*, thou shalt be the companion of the One thou desirest, thou shalt behold in majesty the One thou confessest in His misery; nor do I postpone what I promise, for it is on this very day that thou shalt be with Me." The truly good and sweet Lord Jesus promptly listens, promptly promises, promptly gives. Who could despair of so attentive a Listener, so instant a Promiser, so swift a Giver?

We hope in You, knowing Your sweet name, *for You forsake not those who seek You*. In our mind—the only way possible to us—we come to You, gentle Jesus, seated upon the throne of majesty, and we pray that we may deserve to be admitted to You and by You into the place which the thief entered by confessing You upon the throne of the cross.

Chapter IX—On the Third Leaf of the Vine, or the Third Word of Christ on the Cross

1. The third leaf, and the third chord of the Harp, is the third saying of Jesus: *"Woman, behold thy son";* and *"Behold thy Mother."* Sweet and delightful word! Wonderful word, expressing the deepest filial devotion! Nowhere do we read that the good and kind Jesus remained in His final years in close relationship with His Mother, shared her meals frequently, or addressed her any more affectionately than others. But in these few words, uttered on the brink of death, He did reveal the depth of His love for her. Besides His own suffering on the cross, how great a share of His Mother's suffering must He have borne; for He knew well that now the sword of bitterest sorrow was piercing her gentle heart. He saw the anguish of that heart as she stood there with hands clasped in agony, her eyes bathed in a torrent of tears, her face distorted, and her voice a piteous sob; as she courageously summoned all her strength to face Him on the cross. Beneath her veil—worn, one imagines, out of virginal modesty and because of the depth of her sorrow—how heavily did she grieve and how constantly weep for her Son, saying: "Jesus, my Son Jesus, who will grant me to die with Thee, Jesus, my dearest Son?" How often must she have turned her modest eyes upon those cruel wounds, if, indeed, she turned them away at all, or if she was able to see through the flood of her tears! And how is it that she did not even swoon, when we truly wonder why she did not actually die from the immense pain of her heart? Living, she died with her Son; remaining alive, she suffered a pain worse than death.

2. If she did not faint in this agony, it was because her Son inwardly sustained her, and outwardly comforted her by His consoling word and action. In what manner? As she stood close to the cross, He said to her: *"Behold thy son,"* as if saying: In Me, you shall suffer the bodily loss of a Son; therefore I give you for a son a friend I love above all the others; his presence will console you while I am gone. And you, John, shall lose in Me a Father, so I give you for a mother this Mother I love so much.

How generous You were at Your wedding, O King and Spouse! How generously, O good Jesus, You have given away all Your belongings! For even to the crucifiers You have offered the kindness of Your prayers; to the thief, You have given paradise; to the Mother, a son; to the son, a Mother; to the dead, life;

into the hands of Your Father, Your spirit; to the whole world, the signs of Your power. For the redemption of the slave, You have shed, through Your countless gaping wounds, not a measure but the whole of Your blood; to the one who delivered You up—the traitor—You have given the punishment of his crime;[34] and to the earth, for a time at least, Your incorruptible body.

CHAPTER X—ON THE FOURTH LEAF OF THE VINE, OR THE FOURTH WORD OF CHRIST ON THE CROSS

1. The fourth leaf, and the fourth chord of the Harp, is the fourth word of the Lord, which He uttered *about the ninth hour,* when He *cried out with a loud voice …,* "*Eli, Eli, lema sabacthani,*" that is, "*My God, My God, why hast Thou forsaken Me?*"

Where are the eyes that fail to see this leaf, where the ears that fail to hear this chord? Why, indeed, does He *cry out*, if not to be better heard? How deep must have been the cruel pain of Jesus as these words rang out from His tortured body! But do not be led to believe that the *loud voice* means that Jesus, the Lord most mild, had yielded to impatience. As the next leaf or chord will show, He kept His courage throughout His dreadful passion, although He also revealed the depth of His torment.

2. In saying "My God," Christ manifestly spoke through the humanity He had assumed while remaining the one Person identified with the Son of God; for He who is one God with the Father could not have said such a thing if He had not been also man. Now, what is this He says—"*Why hast Thou forsaken Me*"? Could the Father ever forsake His only-begotten Son? Assuredly not. But our Head, the most loving Jesus, spoke in this way for the whole body, that is, the whole Church. In order to evince His unity with the Church, His bride, and His love for her, He thus made it clear that He would suffer in all her members—He who was suffering as her Head, that is, in His own body, born of the Virgin. Hence, the One who cannot possibly be derelict cries out that He is forsaken, because many of His members are to suffer distress to the point of appearing almost abandoned by God.

Blessed be the lovable Lord, Jesus most kind, who deigns to suffer for us, first in Himself, then with us and in us, regarding as His own our sufferings for justice' sake, and proclaiming, *I will be with him in distress*, so as to strengthen our confidence in Him.

CHAPTER XI—ON THE FIFTH LEAF OF THE VINE, OR THE FIFTH WORD OF CHRIST ON THE CROSS

1. The fifth leaf, and the fifth chord, is the fifth word the most loving Jesus uttered on the cross, saying: "*I thirst*"; whereupon they gave Him wine mixed with myrrh and gall to drink. All other members of the most sweet Jesus' body having been punished, His tongue must now be punished also. In His thirst the vine, turned wild and bitter, offered Him its fruit's bitter juice—not to drink but to taste only, since a mere taste was enough for the tongue's torture.

2. Although this actually happened for the fulfillment of the Scriptures, the word "*I thirst*" seems to have an additional meaning. It appears that, in so speaking, Jesus wanted to express the immensity of His love, for a thirsty man craves for drink much more desperately than a hungry man craves for food. Indicating to us by this thirst the intensity of desire for a thing most ardently sought, Christ gave us a symbolic demonstration of His burning love. In addition, we can accept the fact of His real, literal thirst, for, parched as He was in His whole body from the loss of the sacred blood, *His bones had grown dry like fuel for the fire*. Yet it does not seem probable that He would speak merely of bodily thirst when He

---

[34] We see here an instance of Bonaventure's fondness for series, even loosely bound. In the present case, the bond is merely the fact that a punishment is "given." As an example of generosity, this would be rather surprising.

knew that in a few moments He would suffer bodily death. It seems, rather, that He thirsted with the most intense desire for our salvation.

But there is something else here that should really move us. Earlier, as the hour of His passion was approaching, the most sweet Jesus *fell prostrate and prayed, saying*: "*Father, if it is possible, let this cup pass away from Me.*" He said this not once but a second and a third time; and by the cup He was to drink He meant the passion He was to suffer. Now, having emptied this same cup of the passion, He says: "*I thirst.*" What does He mean?

Before tasting the cup, O good Jesus, You prayed that it might be taken away from You; but now, after emptying it, You thirst. How wonderful this appears! Was Your cup perhaps filled with the wine of delight, instead of humiliation and the worst bitterness? Emphatically not! It was filled with the most withering shame. This should not produce thirst, but rather aversion to drink.

3. When, before You suffered, You prayed that the cup be removed from You, we must believe it was not a refusal of the passion itself. You had come for this very suffering, without which mankind would not have been saved. But it might have been said that, true man though You are, since You are also one with God, the bitterness of the passion did not really affect You. That is why You prayed once, twice, and even three times that the cup be removed from You: to prove to the doubters how supremely bitter was Your suffering.

To us also, who follow Your teaching and Your example, You have shown that, when threatened by danger, be it even for our own good, we can and should pray frequently that God may graciously hold off from us the lashes of His anger; and if we are not spared, that we may bear them with gratitude, patience, courage, and constancy, following Your example in the passion. By praying before You suffered that this cup might be taken away from You, and by saying, after it was emptied: "I thirst," You showed us how immeasurable is Your love. For this seemed to mean: Although My passion was so dreadful that, because of My human sensibility, I prayed to be saved from it, My love for you, O man, triumphed even over the torments of the cross, making Me thirst for more and greater tortures, if need be. For there is no pain I would refuse to suffer for you, for whose redemption *I lay down My life.*

CHAPTER XII—ON THE SIXTH LEAF OF THE VINE, OR THE SIXTH WORD OF CHRIST ON THE CROSS

1. The sixth leaf, and the sixth chord of the Harp, is the sixth word which Jesus, the true and supreme Sweetness, uttered after taking the bitter wine: "*It is consummated!*"

What does this mean? We have seen above that the Lord, *knowing that all things were now accomplished, that the Scripture might be fulfilled* said, "*I thirst.*" Now, after tasting the wine, He says: "*It is consummated!*" This is, in effect, a full consummation and completion of the scriptural prophecy, to wit: *They put gall in My food, and in My thirst they gave Me vinegar to drink;*[35] and thus, *in all the Scriptures the things referring to Himself were brought to pass.*

---

[35] The Quaracchi edition gives only the first half of this quotation, which, in some manuscripts, is found in full as it is given here.

Chapter XIII—On the Seventh Leaf of the Vine, or the Seventh Word of Christ on the Cross

1. The seventh and final leaf of our Vine, and the seventh chord of the Harp, is the final word of our most loving Jesus: "*Father, into Thy hands I commend My spirit.*"

The literal meaning is clear. Yet how is it that this Son, coeternal and consubstantial with the Father, so explicitly commends His soul into the Father's hands? He who had said only a short time before: "*The prince of the world*"—that is, the devil—"*is coming, and in Me he has nothing,*" knew with absolute certainty that His most holy soul already belonged to the Father. But He chose to commend His soul into the Father's hands in order to teach us, who are *but dust and ashes*, to commit our own soul into those eternal hands. Otherwise, upon leaving the body our soul might be seized by that same prince of the world who, alas, would find in us many things belonging to him. Not necessity, therefore, but the giving of example was the reason why He who owed nothing to sin—who, indeed, had come to take away sin—commended into His Father's hands His holy soul when it was about to depart, most pure, from His most pure body.

2. Our Head, with patient perseverance, bore to the end His cruel passion for our sins, until everything foretold of Him in Holy Writ had been fulfilled. So must we who would be members of this Head persevere in the face of all our troubles, until, following our Guide, Jesus most kind, we reach the end of all our tribulations and can trustingly say with Him: "*It is consummated*"; that is: "By Your help, not by my own strength, *I have fought the good fight, I have finished the course, I have kept the faith.*"

Then grant what, according to Your promise, awaits those who acquit themselves rightly in the struggle: the crown of justice which You, the Just Judge, shall give in Your unclouded day—that day in Your courts which is better than a thousand days elsewhere; that day when You shall be the sole and only Sun. O all-benign Jesus Christ, *Sun of Justice* resplendent in Your might, give Yourself as an everlasting reward to those who fought in the battle and kept fighting to the end. May they receive from You the eternal splendor in which they are to rejoice with endless delight. Yet, *whoever perseveres to the end* shall alone attain to this splendor, "for perseverance is what makes a good work endure."

Chapter XIV—On the Third Likeness: That Is, the Flowers of the Vine

1. The Son of God *emptied Himself, taking the nature of a slave.* Planted in our earth, He accepted the deformity of our body, and bore leaves, flowers, and much fruit in order that, as He had been united to our humanity, so He might unite us to His divinity. But since there is no fruit without a flower, our most kind Lord Jesus came to blossom. And what are these flowers but His virtues? So this glorious Vine bloomed in an admirable, striking, and unique way, bringing forth not only flowers of one kind as do other vines or plants, but possessing in Himself the

beauty of all flowers. He was humble as the violet, chaste as the lily, patient and loving as the rose, and abstemious as the crocus. But let us disregard the other flowers and talk about the rose alone.

CHAPTER XV—ON THE RED AND ARDENT ROSE: IN GENERAL

1. On our Vine, Jesus most kind, there blossoms a red and ardent rose: red with the blood of the passion, ardent with the fire of love, roscid with the tears of Jesus most sweet. Jesus all-excelling, our Joy and the joy of the very angels, wept and was sorrowful. As the apostle says: *In the days of His earthly life, with a loud cry and tears, He offered up prayers and supplications to Him who was able to save Him from death, and was heard because of His reverent submission.*

O heart not of flesh but of stone, you hear that this great and all-sovereign Jesus, *in the days of His flesh* that He had assumed for our sake, was drenched with tears; yet you remain dry. O hardened heart, you hear that the One who *shall not be moved forever*, is moved to tears on your behalf, yet you are not moved to tears. Let me apply the fire of His love and the blood of His passion; perhaps they will warm and soften your heart, that you may shed at least tears for Jesus' tears and blood. Let me apply the heavy hammer, let me pierce you with the iron nails, that you may at least be moved. If you are dry as *parched land*, you can readily be softened by the tears of the most sweet Jesus, shed upon your soil. But if the frost of countless crimes has hardened you into rigid stone, the heavy tools must be applied, the hammer of the cross and the iron spikes; so that, as these spikes are driven in, cleaving you apart, you may give forth a saving flow of tears.

2. If you are still unmoved, O callous and impenitent heart, you are harder than the desert rock that yielded abundant water when twice struck by Moses' rod; all the more so since the hammer of the cross should deal a heavier blow than that rod, and the three spikes thrice hammered in should be a means more forcible and effective for striking water than the double rapping of the rod.

If you are still not shaken, having turned hard as a diamond which can be softened only by the blood of a kid, let me offer you the blood both of a "kid"[36] and of *a lamb ... without spot:* our good Jesus. The strength of that copious blood, boiling with the incomparable heat of love, has broken up and leveled the diamond-hard wall of enmity that had been placed between God and man, and had stood for so many thousands of years that neither the Law nor the Prophets—though they smote it with the hammer of manifold precepts and warnings—could bring it down. But as the blood came forth from our kid and lamb, Jesus worthy of all love, not only was a breach made in this wall, but it was leveled to the ground.

Now, the Lord Jesus is called a "kid"—which is an impure animal—because He bore a nature that, in us, is full of the impurities of sin, even though in Him it had nothing of sin. Because of His transcendent purity, on the other hand, He is the Lamb who not only is without sin, but *who takes away the sin of the world.*

3. O heart diamond-hard, immerse yourself in the plenteous blood of our kid and lamb; rest in it and become warm; once warm, be softened; once softened, let flow a fountain of tears. I will therefore seek, and then find, a well-spring of tears in the sorrow, the cross, the nails, and, finally, the scarlet blood, of Jesus most mild. I will consider and I will understand, as much as He grants me to do so, the ruddiness of body and soul of the Lover different from any other, Jesus most loving. For He was ruddy in a twofold way: by nature He was ruddy in the flesh, which properly has a reddish hue; and by the moving power of love He was no less ruddy in the blood of the passion which so often and so profusely covered His body. This repeated shedding of His sacred blood has been explained several times above, Therefore these instances should not be dwelt upon here lest the reader become wearied.

---

[36] See next paragraph.

4. Yet who would weary of this blood except a man all flesh and blood, in whom there is nothing spiritual? Who, wanting to be free of blood, that is, of the sins contracted through flesh and blood, would not desire this most salutary blood of Jesus all-pure? Who, inebriated but once by this most sweet blood that God in His goodness provides for the needy, would not thirst more and more, hearing and understanding the true words of God's Wisdom, the only-begotten Son of the Father, Jesus all-admirable, as He says: "*He who eats of Me will hunger still, he who drinks of Me will thirst for more*"?

In the blood of man there is such natural sweetness, surpassing that of any other animal, that if a wild beast tastes it but once, from then on it will always want to taste it again. Caring no longer for other animals, it will lie in wait for human prey and rush to destruction for the sake of it. If this is true—much more, BECAUSE it is true—how sweet do you think this blood must be, the blood of the Son of Man, true God and true Man, Jesus all sweetness? What? Irrational animals thirst for the blood of man; and shall I not thirst for the blood of the God-and-Man, Jesus who has no peer? The more often wild animals taste human blood, the more they thirst for it; and shall I tire of the blood of the God-and-Man, Jesus most kind? Savage beasts spring to their death in their craving for the sweetness of human blood; and shall I not hasten toward my Life, the blood of Jesus *radiant and ruddy*?

Yes, surely, I will hasten and I will drink; and, *without money and without any price*, I will buy the *wine and milk* which the Wisdom of the Father most high, Jesus all love, has mixed for us in the cup of His body—that is, His blood, the price of our life. All who love the beloved Jesus, *come ye* with me and buy, *not with perishable things, with silver or gold*: through a change in the way you live and act, purchase this wine and milk, the blood most pure, which inebriates the perfect as wine, and nourishes the little ones as milk. For be you perfect and full of strength, the blood of Jesus is for you strong wine straight from the grapes; but be you feeble, and a suckling still, it is for you sustaining milk. Drink, therefore, of this blood most pure.

CHAPTER XVI—ON THE ROSE OF LOVE

1. Having considered the rose in general, let us now consider the rose of love and the rose of the passion. We can measure the ardor of love's rose by carefully considering who this merciful and admirable Lover is, why, what, and how much He loved: He our Lover than whom none is greater, richer, stronger, He of whom every spirit confesses, *Thou art my God*. This expression makes us understand clearly WHO the Lover is: God. The reason WHY He loves us may be gathered from the words that follow: *For Thou hast no need of my goods*. That is, God loved us, not in order to gain anything from us, but out of gratuitous love: and even if there were in us something good that He might desire, it would not be from ourselves but from Him. Now, what we were when He loved us is explained by the apostle, who says: *When we were enemies, we were reconciled to God*. The Just One fell in love with the iniquitous, the Beautiful One with the vile, the only Good and the Holy One with the sinful and unholy. Oh, tremendous condescension! See now HOW MUCH He loved us. Who could explain it well enough?

CHAPTER XVII—ON THE ROSE OF THE PASSION

1. To illustrate how much He loved us, we must connect the rose of the passion with the rose of love. The rose of love will then display its crimson flame in the passion, and the rose of the passion will glow with the fire of love.

Our Lover loved us so much that, pressed by the ardor of His love, He turned scarlet in the passion and delivered Himself to death, *even to death on a cross*; and not merely for a few passing hours, but for the whole time between His birth and His most bitter death. For everything that Jesus all-good endured *in the days of His flesh* is implied in the redness of the rose of pain, although that rose was colored chiefly by His sacred blood, so bountifully shed. While we cannot now describe again His every suffering, we should not be reluctant to speak anew of the salutary outpourings of His blood, in order to impress more deeply upon our mind what should be remembered always.

Chapter XVIII—On the First Shedding of the Blood of Jesus Christ

1. We find the first shedding of blood at the circumcision, when *His name was called Jesus*, as an early mystical sign that He was to be for us a true Jesus, that is, a Saviour, through the effusion of His blood. Let the young listen and understand; let the minds of boys and girls be impressed many times with the early martyrdom of the innocent Jesus. Isaias, speaking of the birth of our most sweet Lord, says: *A Child is born to us, and a Son is given to us, and the government is upon His shoulder*. Thus he immediately connects the cross, indicated by the word "government," with the nativity, for the crucifixion of Jesus actually began at His birth. It is a momentous indication of His crimson passion that our Lord should have been born in a strange place, in midwinter, in the depth of the night, outside the inn, of a Mother humble and poor. And although at this time there was no shedding of His blood, it did come about after only seven days had passed.

2. Oh, how noble an attestation of love! Hardly has heaven's Glory, Wealth, and Joy, the most sweet and loving Infant Jesus, come to life, when behold! the shame, the pain, and the boundless poverty of the cross are at once attached to the new-born Child. But the just designation "government" offsets the humiliation of the cross. Jesus the Mighty One, reigning from the cross, prevailed by the cross over the whole world and over hell; through the cross *He humbled Himself, becoming obedient* to the Father to *death*. Therefore God the Father *also has exalted Him and has bestowed upon Him the Name that is above every name*.

This name, Jesus, was fittingly applied at the first shedding of the blood of the Lamb most pure. It was for our salvation that the first drop of this blood was shed, the blood which, to fulfill our salvation, was to be poured out in full.

Chapter XIX—On the Second Shedding of Blood

1. The second shedding of the blood of Jesus most sweet which gave the rose of the passion its crimson color, consists in the sweat of blood of Christ praying in agony. *Falling into an agony He prayed the more earnestly. And His sweat became as drops of blood running down upon the ground.*

Even supposing that no more blood was to be shed, would not this one instance have sufficed to redden our rose? Beyond doubt. Tremble with fear and break, my wretched heart; be flooded with tears of blood. See: a sweat of blood covers my Creator; and it does not merely trickle drop by drop, but pours down to the ground.

Woe to the ignoble heart which, even under so marvelous a laving, still remains dry. Consider the distress which tormented that heart most mild as the effusion of blood dripped from every pore of the whole body. Would the body have given forth externally such a wondrous super-flux if the heart had not been broken internally under the pressure of sorrow? As the prophet has said: *My heart is broken within Me*. Now that the heart is riven within, the skin of the true Solomon, the most loving Jesus, is opened without, and the bloody sweat runs down to the ground. Reddened is the rose of the love and passion of Christ, the ruddy Jesus; Jesus ruddy through and through.

2. It is not without a mysterious significance that the whole body of Jesus the all-good was covered with blood. Since He came to take away the weaknesses we had contracted through our body and our blood, His whole body sweated blood. The bloody sweat pouring forth as it did from every part of the body of Jesus our Head, sealed and healed the wounds of the whole spiritual body, that is, the Church. Thus we have been freed from bloodguilt by the God of our Salvation, Jesus most kind, who bled for our sake. Also, this

sweat of blood assuredly signified that throughout the whole body, that is, the Church, or spiritual body, the blood of martyrs was to be shed and the Church itself was to receive a scarlet hue.

CHAPTER XX—ON THE THIRD SHEDDING OF BLOOD

1. The third shedding of blood occurred when they plucked His cheeks, as the prophet testifies speaking in the person of the lovable Lord Jesus: *I have given My body to the strikers, and My cheeks to them that plucked them.* Some interpret this to mean that the wicked Jews tore His face with their fingernails; others, that they plucked His beard. Neither could have been done without the shedding of blood.

I see the sacrilegious hands of this most impious mob, who are not content with striking, slapping, and covering with spittle the adorable face of Jesus all-good, but now, in their burning rage, also pluck His cheeks and draw from that most sweet face the blood which reddens our rose. I see in this *Lamb without blemish* a patience worthy of admiration and imitation, as He turns in all meekness His cheeks most pure to the harrowing of impure claws; so that, if ever shame should cover our own face for His sake, we may suffer patiently.

CHAPTER XXI—ON THE FOURTH SHEDDING OF BLOOD[37]

1. The fourth shedding of blood occurred when the cruel crown of thorns was set, not gently but with vengeful force, upon the most sweet head of our Jesus. Indeed, it seems manifest that those who hated Truth sought not only to insult Him but also to injure Him. Nor can it be thought that there was no blood shed here. Instead, from the head so derisively and spitefully crowned, rivers of blood flowed down upon the face and the neck of Jesus most sweet. If these men had not intended to inflict upon the One they crowned torture as well as mockery, they would have used shoots or twigs of some other tree to plait the crown. But as an evidence of their cruelty, they crowned with piercing thorns the Lamb most mild, the Lord Jesus, who is now *crowned … with glory and honor.* Although the crowning was to be in sport, the sport-makers unwittingly confess their victim to be a King, since only kings are crowned. Knowing Him not, they prove that He is King, but crowning Him, they prove their own malice through the thorns.

CHAPTER XXII—ON THE FIFTH SHEDDING OF BLOOD

1. The fifth shedding of blood occurred at the scourging of the Lamb most mild, the crimsoned Jesus, Oh, what a sea of the sacred blood must have soaked the ground from the body of Christ torn by these whips! Oh, how ferocious the rage, how raging the ferocity, with which they scourged the sweet Jesus, who had come precisely to save us from the eternal scourge! "They have fallen upon Me with scourges without cause." Without cause, indeed, unless these ungodly and wicked men, by turning truth into a lie, found that Your good works deserved punishment.

2. All this contains a moral lesson. It teaches us how to bear with courageous patience the scourgings inflicted by our blessed Father, as our Lord Jesus most sweet so patiently bore for us unworthy ones the scourgings of the iniquitous. Seeing how the *King of kings and Lord of lords,* Jesus most loving, who was free from all sin and in whose mouth no deceit was found, is martyred by such savage stripes, what scourge would a man refuse to suffer, *born,* as he is, *to labor,* nurtured in sin, living in sin, yet destined to inherit the heavenly kingdom unto which none but the pure attain? O man, foolish and without understanding, hear and be instructed. Far from

---

[37] In the Gospel accounts, the scourging precedes the crowning.

trying to flee the discipline, you should rather embrace it, lest you perish from the way of righteousness in the face of the wrath of your Lord, *who has not spared even His own Son but has delivered Him* to be scourged for you.

Chapter XXIII—On the Sixth and Seventh Sheddings of Blood

1. The sixth and most abundant shedding of blood was caused by the piercing nails. Who can doubt that a profuse flow of the sacred blood gushed forth from the hands and feet of the innocent Jesus as they were wounded, pierced through and through? Let the torrents of this blood crimson our rose, for here is love the most ardent, and passion the reddest in its glow. It is in this depth of the passion that we should see the depth of the love; in this redness of the passion that we should see the fire of the rose of love. Who, indeed, has ever suffered such pain and such disgrace? God is the One who suffers; yet He who so often removed or reduced the pressure of His servants' pains in no way eases the pressure of the passion's wine press. The One who knew how to spare His own did not spare Himself. The proof of this is found in the Gospel of John: when those who came to seize Him said that He was the One they sought, He declared: "*I am He. If, therefore, you seek Me, let these go their way.*"

Oh, what fire of true, of truest love! Love in Person reveals and delivers Himself to His raging enemies. While not sparing Himself, He begs that His own may be spared. Captured, our Saviour most mild, Jesus the beloved, is repeatedly ridiculed by both Jews and Gentiles, repeatedly sheds His blood; then both His hands and feet are pierced with spikes and He is nailed to the wood of the cross.

Look and see the rose of the bloody passion; see how it glows as a sign of the most ardent love. Love and the passion are vying: the one to be more ardent, the other more crimson. But, oh, marvel: the passion is reddened with the intensity of love, for Christ would not suffer if He did not love; and in the passion, in the very redness of the passion, the ardor of the greatest and most incomparable love is revealed. For as the rose throughout the chill of night is closed, but in the warmth of the rising sun unfurls again in full and opens up its crimson petals as a sign of flaming joy, so the delight-giving Flower of heaven, Jesus most beautiful—long closed as in the cold of night by Adam's sin, and still withholding from sinners the plenitude of grace—blazes anew in the *fullness of time* with the flames of a burning love, opens up in every wounded limb, and reveals in the glow of flowing blood the refulgence of the rose of charity.[38]

2. Behold how the crimsoned Jesus blossomed forth in this rose. See His whole body: is there a single spot where the rose is not found? Examine one hand, then the other; examine one foot and then the other; and see whether you do not find the roses. Examine the wound of His side, for the rose is still there, although of a paler red because of the admixture of water; for *there came out blood and water*. Indeed, *this is He who came in water and in blood*, Christ Jesus the all-good.

O most sweet Lord and Saviour of men, O good Jesus, how can I give worthy thanks to You who, from the dawn of Your life to Your cruel death, and even after it, have shed for me so much of Your blood; to You who desired to reveal the fire of Your surpassing love by shedding Your blood so often? How manifold and well adorned is this Rose with its innumerable petals! Who could count them all? Number the drops of blood that ran from the sweet wounds of the side and the body of the most loving Jesus, and you have

---

[38] This poetical passage deserves to be quoted in full in the original Latin: "Sicut enim rosa per frigus noctis clausa, solis ardore surgente, tota aperitur et foliis expansis in rubore demonstrat ardorem iucundum; ita flos caeli deliciosus, optimus Iesus, qui multo tempore a peccato primi hominis quasi in frigore noctis clausus fuit, peccatoribus nondum gratiae plenitudinem impendens, tandem plenitudine temporis accedente, radiis ardentis caritatis accensus, in omni corporis sui parte apertus est, et rosae caritatis ardor in rubore sanguinis effusi refulsit."

counted the petals of the rose of suffering and love, for every single drop of blood is another petal.

Of the Lord's seventh shedding of blood we have already briefly spoken, when we said that from the opening in His side *there came out blood and water.* In this are signified the mysteries of baptism.

Chapter XXIV—Exhortation to Contemplate the Passion and the Love of Christ

1. Be strong, then, my weak and wretched soul, and rise aloft; on the wings of faith and hope, fly to this garden of love; concentrate the scattered vision of your mind, and follow the zeal of the bee in gathering for yourself the honey of devotion. Rise to the paradise of love—rise, I say, to the heights of the heart; behold, the One you seek has been lifted up.

But have no fear: being exalted, He was humbled. For He was not lifted up on the cross to show Himself less accessible to those who seek Him, but in very truth to make Himself more accessible to all. And as you approach this paradise with trusting heart, feel the love of the Crucified expressed by the open arms, feel the embrace of Him who offers Himself to you and calls you, and who, wondrously combining misery with mercy, exclaims: "*Turn, turn, O Sulamite, turn, turn, that we may look at you.*" Turn away from your evil will, from your evil deeds, from your obstinacy and despair; turn back to Me, for you have turned away from Me. Let Me look upon you with the eyes of grace wherewith I looked upon the sinful woman and upon the thief.

2. I am the *Scroll written within and without:* read Me and understand Whom you read. Gather the flowers of My wounds so that you may enter their garden of delight, before whose gate stands the Cherub with the flaming sword. The wisdom you may fully learn of Me is mighty enough to disarm the Cherub, for the flowers of blood extinguish the flames of the burning sword. Enter, O soul, this garden more choice than any other; enter it through your loving meditation—the only way open for you now—so that later you may be admitted, soul and body, into the heavenly paradise.

To view this garden in a brief glance is not enough: we must go from blossom to blossom and draw nectar from each separate flower; now at the right side, now at the left, we must try to approach ever more intimately and closely the flowing streams of blood. Everywhere we are to seek devotion and the grace of tearful repentance; at every wound we are to weigh how cruel are those tearing nails; how bitter the pain of the broken veins and muscles[39] in the hands of the Maker of heaven and earth; how *He hath wrought salvation in the midst of the earth.* While considering these things, let us often repeat: *Give me back the joy of your salvation,* imitating in this way the bee that always sings in flight and is never silent until it enters a flower, where it gathers and absorbs the coveted sweetness.

What happiness for you, when, being let in among the flowers of blood, the wounds of Christ, our blossoming garden of supreme sweetness, you can be completely rid of the world's clamor and the assaults of temptation, and caring now for Him alone whom you have come to meet, can taste and understand how good and sweet He is.

We should also look upon the feet of Christ, for they are no less covered with blood, nor do they suffer less, than the hands. They, too, are wounded and pierced through, spattered with drops and running with streams of blood.

3. Finally, through the open door of His spear-torn side, we should come to the most humble heart of Jesus most high. Here, in all truth, is hidden the very treasure of love, desirable and ineffable; here we discover devotion, and the grace of tears; here we learn benignity and patience in our afflictions, and compassion for the afflicted; here, above all, we find within ourselves *a heart contrite and humbled.*

---

[39] The Latin has "ossium" (bones), which seems to contradict the traditional interpretation of Ps. 33:21: *He watches over all His bones; not one of them shall be broken.*

The One so good and so great desires you to embrace Him and is waiting to embrace you. He inclines toward you the flower of His head, pierced with many thorns, and calls you to receive the kiss of peace, as if saying: See how I was disfigured, transfixed, and beaten in order that I might place you upon My shoulder, My straying sheep, and bring you back to the paradise of heavenly pastures. Do something now yourself: be moved with pity for My wounds; and such as you see Me, *set Me as a seal on your heart, as a seal on your arm*; so that, in every motion of your heart, in every deed of your hands, you may resemble Me who am wearing the seals you behold. In forming you, I conformed you to the likeness of My divinity; to re-form you, I conformed Myself to the likeness of your humanity. Do you, who did not keep the imprint of My divinity stamped on you when you were made, keep at least the imprint of your own humanity stamped on Me when you were re-formed. If you did not stay as I created you, stay at least as I re-created you. If you fail to understand how great were the powers I granted you in creating you, understand at least how great were the miseries I accepted for you in your humanity, in re-creating you, and in re-forming you for joys much greater than those for which I had originally formed you. I became human and visible so that you might see Me and so love Me, since, unseen and invisible in My divinity, I had not been properly loved. As a price for My incarnation and passion, give Me yourself, for whom I became flesh and for whom I suffered. I gave Myself to you, now give yourself to Me.

4. O most sweet and good Jesus, *Father of Lights*, from whom proceeds *every good gift and every perfect gift*, look down mercifully upon us who humbly confess You and truly know that we can do nothing without Your help. You gave Yourself in payment for us; grant that, although we are little worthy of such a price, we may be so completely and fully restored to Your favor that, conforming to the image of Your passion, we may also be re-formed to the image of Your divinity.

May God grant it to us. Amen.

On the Perfection of Life Addressed to Sisters

De perfectione vitae ad sorores

An Outline of Spiritual Progress

Prologue

HAPPY THE MAN *whom You instruct, O Lord, whom by Your Law You teach*. No one, admittedly, is to be esteemed wise save only him who is taught by the unction of the Spirit. This is why the Prophet David says that he alone is truly happy and wise whose mind the Lord instructs, and whose soul He teaches by His law. For the law of the Lord is the only law without stain, the only blameless law, the only one that converts souls to salvation. Now, the teaching or the knowledge of this law is to be sought, not so much externally in its letter, but rather through a devout movement of the mind. It is to be longed after in spirit and *in power*, so as to let Him teach interiorly who alone can change the exterior harshness of the law into inner sweetness.

The law of the Lord teaches us what to do and what to avoid, what to believe and what to pray for, what to desire and what to fear; it teaches us to be immaculate and blameless, to fulfill our promises and weep for our sins, to despise the things of the world and reject the things of the flesh; finally, it teaches us to turn with our whole heart, our whole soul, our whole mind, to Jesus Christ alone. Beside this doctrine, all the wisdom of the world is foolish and vain. Bernard writes: "Others may, if they will, call a man wise, even though he fears not God and loves Him not. I never would." He is truly wise and happy who is not a forgetful hearer of this teaching, but its faithful doer. Therefore, as the psalmist says, *happy the man whom You instruct, O Lord, whom by Your Law You teach*.

2. For this reason, reverend Mother, devoted to God and dear to me, you have asked me to dictate, out of the poverty of my heart, a treatise in which your soul may find some timely thoughts to nourish its devotion. But I must confess I am so poorly equipped that I need rather to be taught myself, especially since, in my case, reputation is not brilliant abroad, nor is devotion aflame within, nor does knowledge come to my aid. Yet, moved by your eager and holy request, I shall try to be as humble in obeying as you were insistent in making it. I beg that your kindness, very holy Mother, will regard the sincerity of my intentions rather than the actual accomplishment; the truth of the words rather than the quality of the style. And if, because of scant leisure and pressing duties, I fail to meet your expectations, I beg you to be indulgent and forgive me.

I begin with the chapter titles, which should help you to find without difficulty what you seek.

I. On True Self-Knowledge

II. On True Humility

III. On Perfect Poverty

IV. On Silence and Quiet

V. On Assiduity in Prayer

VI. On Remembering the Passion of Christ

VII. On Perfect Love for God

VIII. On Final Perseverance

MYSTICAL OPOSCULA

CHAPTER I—ON TRUE SELF-KNOWLEDGE

1. First of all, the bride of Christ who wishes to rise to the summit of perfect life should start at the level of her own self. Forgetting the material world, she must enter the hidden recesses of her conscience, there to explore, examine, and weigh with attentive care all her faults, habits, affections, and deeds; all her sins, both past and present. Whatever fault she finds within herself, let her repent it with sincere grief.

A good way to self-knowledge, dear Mother, is to realize that we commit all our sins and wrong actions through either negligence, or concupiscence, or malice. So whenever you think of your past sins, you should bear these three things in mind; otherwise you will never acquire perfect self-knowledge.

2. If you desire to know yourself, therefore—and through this knowledge, to feel true compunction for your sins—you should first consider whether you are, or ever have been, NEGLIGENT. In other words, ask yourself in what degree you fail to guard your heart, or to make good use of your time, or what wrong purpose you may have in your work. Be sure always to guard your heart well, to spend your time usefully, and to assign a good and fitting end to all your deeds.

Think also whether you are negligent in reading, praying, or working. If you would bring forth good fruit in due season, you must diligently train and exercise yourself in all three of these pursuits, for any one of them is not enough without the others. In addition, observe to what extent you are, or may have been, negligent in doing penance, in resisting evil, or in making spiritual progress. You must earnestly deplore your sins, reject all diabolical temptations, and proceed from one virtue to another until you reach the promised land.

This is the proper way to meditate upon negligence.

3. Secondly, if you desire to know yourself better, you should search inwardly to learn whether the CONCUPISCENCE of pleasure, of curiosity, or of vanity is, or ever was, alive in you.

Certainly, the concupiscence of pleasure is alive in a religious who craves for sweet things, like dainty food, or things pleasant to the touch, like fine clothes, or carnal things, like lustful satisfaction.

The concupiscence of curiosity is alive in the handmaid of God who desires to know what should remain unknown, to see seductive beauty, and to possess uncommon objects.

The concupiscence of vanity is alive in the bride of Christ who seeks worldly favor, yearns for worldly praise, and craves for worldly honor. The handmaid of Christ should spurn such things as she would a deadly poison, for they are the roots of every evil.

4. Thirdly, if you desire to know yourself very well, you should diligently investigate whether the MALICE of anger, of envy, or of spiritual boredom is, or ever was, alive in you.

Anger is alive within the religious through movements of the heart, feelings, or emotions; or outwardly, by signs, gestures, words, or exclamations that manifest even the slightest indignation or bitterness toward the neighbor.

Envy reigns in one to whom the neighbor's woe is joy and the neighbor's joy is woe; to whom the neighbor's delight means pain, and the neighbor's pain, delight.

Spiritual boredom vitiates the heart of one who in the religious life is lukewarm, half-awake, slow, lazy, slack, unfervent, disgusted. The bride of Christ should detest these vices and avoid them as deadly poison, for they are the undoing of both body and soul.

5. Therefore, handmaid beloved of God, if you would know yourself perfectly, "return to your own self, enter into your heart, learn the value of your soul, ponder what you were, are, should have been, and can be: what you were by nature, what you now are through sin, what you should have been through effort, and what you still can be through grace."

"Listen, Mother, listen to the prophet David offering himself as an example to you: *In the night, I meditate in my heart; I ponder, and my spirit broods.* He meditated in his heart: do you also meditate in your heart. His spirit brooded: let your spirit also brood. Plow this field, work on yourself. If you persevere in this work, you will surely discover a precious hidden treasure. This work will make your wealth of gold increase, your knowledge widen, your wisdom grow. This work will wipe your inner vision clean, sharpen your mind, broaden your understanding. Lack of self-knowledge and failure to appreciate one's own worth make for faulty judgment in all other matters. The man who does not first meditate upon his own spirit will not know at all what to think of the spirit of the angels and the spirit of God. As long as you are unable to understand your own self, how should you be able to understand what is above you? As long as you are unworthy of entering the first tabernacle, how should you presume to enter the second?"

6. If you wish to rise to the second and third heavens, you must go through the first, that is, your heart. I have already sufficiently explained how you can and should do this; but blessed Bernard also gives some excellent advice when he says: "As an inquisitive explorer of your spiritual health, examine and analyze your life thoroughly. Make a careful reckoning of how far you have advanced and how far you have to go, how well you behave and how wisely you love, how like you are to God or how unlike Him, how close you are to God or how far removed from Him."

Oh, how dangerous it is for a religious to be inquisitive about many things while ignoring her own self! Oh, how close that religious comes to perdition and ruin who, curious about everything, and busily judging the consciences of others, knows nothing at all about herself! O my God, whence such blindness in one dedicated to You? Yet the reason is obvious: the human mind, distracted by worldly cares, fails to enter into itself through memory; clouded by imagination, it fails to turn toward itself through intelligence; attracted by concupiscence, it fails to return to itself through desire for inner sweetness and spiritual joy. Therefore, totally immersed in the senses, it is unable to re-enter into itself as into the likeness of God. Thus, the mind, wholly wretched, knows nothing about itself.

So, putting everything else aside, apply your intellect and memory to yourself. Blessed Bernard himself prayed for this, saying: "God grant to me to have no other knowledge than the understanding of myself."

CHAPTER II—ON TRUE HUMILITY

1. She who would see her own defects through the eye of the heart must truly humble herself *under the mighty hand of God*. So, handmaid of Christ, once you have obtained knowledge of your own defects, I counsel you to humble your spirit deeply, and to deem yourself worthless. "For humility," says blessed Bernard, "is the virtue by which a man, knowing well what he is, deems himself worthless."

This is the kind of humility that led our blessed father Francis to pass such severe judgment upon himself; the humility he loved and cultivated from the beginning of his religious life until his death; the humility which prompted him to leave the world, to ask his brethren that he be dragged, stripped of his outer garments, through the public square; the humility which made him serve lepers, reveal his past sins in his sermons, and beg his brethren to reproach him.

O Mother devoted to God, you should learn this virtue primarily from the Son of God, for He Himself has said: "*Learn from Me, for I am meek and humble of heart.*" In the words of blessed Gregory: "Gathering virtues without humility is like carrying dust in the wind." *Pride is the beginning of all sin*; and equally, humility is the foundation of all virtue.

Learn to be truly humble, rather than falsely so, like those hypocrites who abase themselves to deceive, as Sirach says: *There is the wicked man who is bowed in grief, but is full of guile within.* "The truly humble man," says blessed Bernard, "wishes to be regarded as worthless, not hailed as an example of humility."

2. So, dearest Mother, if you desire to be perfectly humble, walk along a triple path.

The FIRST PATH is the contemplation of God. You should always see God as the Author of all good. Because He is the Author of all good, we must say to Him: "*Lord, … Thou hast wrought all our works for us.*" For the same reason, you must refer all good to Him, and none to yourself, remembering that it is not your own power and the strength of your own hand that has obtained for you this wealth—for *He made us, and not we ourselves*. This realization totally destroys such pride as would claim: "*Our own hand won the victory; the Lord had nothing to do with it."* Such was the pride that shut Lucifer out from the glory of heaven. Disregarding the knowledge that he came from nothingness, concentrating instead on his own beauty and splendor, and seeing that *every precious stone* was his covering, he was exalted by the pride of his heart. And since humiliation follows the proud, he was immediately hurled from the throne of his glory into a place of utter disgrace; once the best of all angels, he now became the worst of all demons.

3. How many today are Lucifer's followers, men and women who imitate him, sons and daughters of pride! The Lord bears with them patiently, even though "pride would be more easily tolerable in the rich than in the poor," as Bernard says in a sermon on the Canticle. So, if she is to take the place of the expelled angel, the handmaid of Christ must always be found very humble. Whether in angel or in man, only humility is pleasing to God. Do not think that virginity without humility pleases Him. Assuredly, Mary herself would not have become the Mother of God had she been proud. For so blessed Bernard says: "I am not afraid to declare that without humility not even Mary's virginity would have been pleasing to God." Therefore, humility is a great virtue. In its absence, virtue is worse than non-existent: it degenerates into pride.

4. The SECOND PATH consists in remembering Christ. You must call to mind that Christ was humbled to the point of suffering a most infamous death; that He became so lowly as to be compared to a leper. Thus speaks the prophet Isaias: *We have thought Him as it were a leper, and as One struck by God and afflicted*—so much so that, in His own time, no one was thought to be lowlier than He. Isaias also says: *He was taken away from distress and from judgment*, as if meaning: Such was His humiliation, and so low did He Himself descend, that no one would take Him for what He was, no one would believe Him to be God. Our Lord and Master Himself chooses to say: "*No servant is greater than his master, nor is one who is sent greater than he who sent him.*" If you are truly the handmaid of Christ, you must be lowly, contemptible, and humble.

How abominable to God is the religious who displays a humble dress that hides a prideful heart! How unprofitable is the Christian who, while seeing his Lord humbled and despised, is himself arrogant in spirit, and busy with great matters, and with things above him. When the Highest has become the lowest and the Immeasurable has become as tiny as man, what could be more detestable in the bride of Christ, what would deserve a heavier punishment in His handmaid, than for decay and worms to presume to magnify themselves? Of such does blessed Augustine say: "O carrion hide, why such bloating? O foul corruption, why such swelling? Can the head be humble and the body proud?" And he means it should not be so.

5. The THIRD PATH you must follow if you wish to be perfectly humble is self-examination. Self-examination, most beloved Mother, means asking yourself whence you are and whither you are going.

Consider first whence you are, and know that you were made of the matter of perdition, the dust and slime of the earth; that you have kept company with sin, and thus are exiled from the garden of delight. Such meditation rules out and expels the spirit of pride so thoroughly that you will cry out with the three children quoted by Daniel: "*We, O Lord, ... are brought low in all the earth this day for our sins.*"

Consider also whither you are going: straight unto dissolution and cinders, *for dust you are and unto dust you shall return*. Why such pride in one who is but earth and ashes? Alive today, you may be dead tomorrow; wise today, you may be foolish tomorrow; rich and mighty today, you may be a poor beggar tomorrow. What Christian could be so besotted as to swell with pride while seeing himself liable to so many miseries and ills?

6. Learn, O consecrated virgins, to have a humble spirit, a humble bearing, a humble heart, a humble disposition. Only humility appeases God's anger and discovers God's grace. As Sirach says, *humble yourself the more, the greater you are, and you will find favor with God*. Thus did Mary find favor with the Lord, as she herself bears witness when she says: "*Because He has regarded the lowliness of His handmaid.*" No marvel, since humility furnishes a dwelling place for

love, and rids the soul of vanities. Augustine says: "The less we are stuffed with pride, the more we shall be filled with love." As water gathers in the valley, so the graces of the Holy Spirit gather in humble souls; and as water rushes faster down a steeper slope, so the man whose heart is truly humbled reaches the Lord more easily, to receive His grace more fully. Sirach says: *The prayer of the lowly pierces the clouds; it does not rest till it reaches its goal*, for the Lord *fulfills the desire of those who fear Him, He hears their cry and saves them.*

7. Handmaid of God, servant of Christ, be humble so as *never to suffer pride to reign in thy mind*. You have a humble Teacher, our Lord Jesus Christ, and you have a humble model, the Virgin Mary, Queen of all. Be humble, for you have a humble father, blessed Francis; be humble, for you have a humble mother, blessed Clare, a mirror of humility. Yet be humble in such a way that your patience is the proof of your humility. The virtue of humility is made perfect by forbearance, and without forbearance there is no true humility. Blessed Augustine explains this well: "It is easy to cover your face with a veil, to wear cheap and lowly clothes, to walk about with your head bent low, but the proof of true humility is forbearance." In this, he follows the words of Ecclesiasticus: *In thy humiliation, keep patience.*

I must sadly admit that many of us who were nothing in the world want to be important in the monastery. Wherefore, blessed Bernard says: "I am sorry to see not a few religious who spurned the pride of the world, now learning pride in the school of humility. Although tutored by a Master meek and humble, they grow more overbearing and impatient in the cloister than they had ever been in the world. What is even worse, there are many in the house of God who cannot bear humiliation, although in their own household they held nothing but the lowest place."

8. I advise you, therefore, dear Mother, to tell the virgins consecrated to God who are your daughters, that they are to safeguard humility in their virginal state, and virginity in a humble soul. For virginity combined with humility is like a gem set in gold. Blessed Bernard says: "Beautiful is the union of virginity and humility. Pleasing to God is the soul in which humility enhances virginity, and virginity adorns humility."

Finally, listen to my brotherly advice; listen, Mother, and you will agree. Flee the daughters of pride like vipers; avoid the proud virgins like demons; shun the company of the prideful like deadly poison. And why should you do this? I will tell you why. A wise man has described the proud in these words: "The proud man is impatient; he is overdressed; he walks pompously and looks down his nose; his face is grim and his eyes spell murder; he fights for the first place and wants to be put ahead of the best; his opinions, words, and actions are arrogant; politeness is foreign to him." Handmaid of God, bride of Christ, virgin of the Lord, you must flee the company of the proud lest you become like them. For, as Ecclesiasticus says: *He that hath fellowship with the proud shall put on pride.*

CHAPTER III—ON PERFECT POVERTY

1. The virtue of poverty is needed also for the fullness of perfection. It is impossible to attain the perfect life without it, as the Lord teaches in the Gospel: "*If thou wilt be perfect, go, sell what thou hast, and give to the poor.*" Since the summit of evangelical perfection consists in supreme poverty, let no one imagine that he has attained the peak of virtue if he is not yet an exact observer of evangelical poverty. Hugh of St. Victor says: "However perfect religious may be, their perfection is not to be considered full unless they also love poverty."

2. Two things should move every religious, and in fact every soul, toward the love of poverty: one is the divine example, which is beyond reproach; the other is the divine promise, which is beyond price. The first thing that should move you, handmaid of Christ, toward the love of poverty, is love for our Lord Jesus Christ and the example He gave: for He was born poor, He lived poor, and He died poor.

3. See what a model of poverty He left you, that by His example, you also might become a friend of poverty. Our Lord Jesus Christ was so poor at birth that He had no decent roof, no dainty robes, no rich nourishment. For shelter He had a stable; to cover Him, plain swaddling clothes; and for food, the milk of a Virgin. The apostle Paul was so moved at the thought of these privations that he wrote to the Corinthians: *Being rich, He became poor for your sakes, that by His poverty you might become rich.* And blessed Bernard says: "Heaven was rich with the eternal wealth of all goods, but poverty was missing. On earth, this commodity abounded and superabounded, and man did not know its worth. The Son of God, desiring to obtain it, came down from heaven to embrace it, and to make it precious for us by appraising it so high."

4. The Lord Jesus Christ, through His way of life on earth, gave Himself as an example of poverty to us. Dear Sister—and all of you who profess poverty—listen to how poor the Son of God and the King of angels was while He lived on earth. He was so poor that sometimes He did not have shelter; He and His apostles often had to sleep in the fields outside the town or village. The evangelist Mark writes: *And when He had looked round upon all things, then, as it was already late, He went out to Bethany with the Twelve.* The gloss says here: "*He had looked round* to see if anyone would accommodate Him; but His poverty was so great, and He was appreciated by so few, that He could not find shelter in that large city." And Matthew quotes Him thus: "*The foxes have dens, and the birds of the air have nests; but the Son of Man has nowhere to lay His head.*"

5. Not only was the Lord of angels poor at the time of His birth, not only was He poor in His way of life, but He became poorer than ever in death, to inflame us with love for the same poverty. O all ye who profess poverty, *attend, and see* how poor in death this rich King of heaven became for our sake. He was despoiled and stripped of everything. His clothing was taken when *they divided His garments among them, and upon His vesture they cast lots.* His body and His life were taken when, in the bitter pain of death, His spirit left His flesh. He was even robbed of His divine glory when *they did not glorify Him as God,* but treated Him as a criminal; as was foretold by Job in the prophetic complaint: *He has stripped me of my glory.* Blessed Bernard summarizes this example of the greatest need: "See the poor Christ, born without decent shelter, lying in a manger between an ox and an ass, wrapped in poor swaddling clothes, fleeing into Egypt, riding an ass, and hanging naked upon a gibbet."

6. What Christian is so unworthy, what religious so hopelessly hard-hearted, as to cling to love of wealth and hatred of poverty while seeing and hearing the God of gods, the Lord of the universe, the King of heaven, the only-begotten Son of God, under the burden of such absolute want? "It is a great abuse," as blessed Bernard says, "a very great abuse, that desire for wealth should move such a vile worm, for whose sake the God of majesty, the Lord of Sabaoth, willed to become poor." "Let the pagan seek wealth, for he lives without God; let the Jew seek wealth, for he was promised abundance on earth." But as for you, virgin of Christ and handmaid of the Lord, why would you seek wealth? Have you not vowed to be poor, to live among the poor of Christ, and to be the daughter of a poor father, Francis, and the follower of a poor mother, Clare? Indeed, dearest Mother, we profess poverty, but practice greed instead; we seek what is not permitted, and desire what the rule forbids. This greed of ours—mine as well as yours—was emphatically put to shame when the Son of God became poor for our sake.

7. I know it to be a fact that the more fervently you love the poverty you profess, and the more perfectly you practice the poverty of the Gospel, the more you will abound in goods both temporal and spiritual. But if you turn to the opposite course, if you despise this poverty you profess, you will be wanting in goods both temporal and spiritual. Mary, the poor Mother of the poor Christ, once said: *He has filled the hungry with good things, and the rich He has sent away empty.* And the holy prophet foretold the same: *The great grow poor and hungry; but those who seek the Lord want for no good thing.* Have you not heard, have you not read, what our Lord Jesus Christ said to His apostles, as told in the Gospel of Matthew:

"*Therefore do not be anxious, saying, 'What shall we eat?' or 'What shall we drink?' … for your Father knows that you need all these things*"? Listen again to what He asks them, in the Gospel of Luke: "*When I sent you forth without purse or wallet or sandals, did you lack anything?" And they said, "Nothing.*" If, therefore, the Lord took such good care of His disciples among the unbelievers and the hard-hearted Jews without their having to be concerned at all, why marvel that He provides for the Friars Minor who profess the same perfection, or for the poor Sisters who imitate the evangelical poverty, when these live among believing Christians? *Cast all your anxiety upon Him, because He cares for you.*

8. Since the Father surrounds us with such great solicitude, since He takes such good care of us, it seems amazing that we should be so deeply concerned about the frivolous and perishable things of this world. I find no other cause for this than greed, the mother of confusion and damnation; I can discover no other reason than that our affections have strayed far away from God, our Salvation; I can see no other explanation than that our love for God has turned to frost and ice within us. Most certainly, if we were burning with love, we would shed our worldly garments to follow the naked Christ. Those who feel very hot take off their clothes. It is a sign of great coldness in us that we should snatch so eagerly at these perishable things.

O my God! How can we be so hard toward Christ, who left His country—heaven; His kinsfolk—the angels; and the house of His Father, meaning His Father's glory, and became poor, humiliated, and despised, for us? How is it possible that we should be unwilling to abandon, for Him, this one world, miserable and rotten as it is? We renounce the world externally, yes. But alas, our whole heart, our whole mind, all our desires are engaged and absorbed in it.

9. Blessed servant of God, remember the poverty of our poor Lord Jesus Christ; impress upon your heart the poverty of your poor father Francis; recall the poverty of your poor mother Clare. With the greatest resolution and effort, adhere to poverty, embrace Lady Poverty, and in the name of the Lord do not love anything under the sun except poverty: neither honors, nor temporal goods, nor wealth; but be sure to observe with the greatest firmness the poverty you promised to follow.

Vain it is to love the wealth we have; dangerous, to love that which we do not have; painful, to have that which we do not love. Hence, neither possession nor love of riches is useful, safe, enjoyable, or an act of perfect virtue. Therefore, the Lord's counsel on poverty, as well as His example, should move all Christians and inflame them with love for such poverty. O blessed poverty, how beloved by God, how safe in the world, do you make those who love you! For, as Gregory says, "the man who has no worldly love will have no worldly fear."

We read in the Lives of the Fathers that a certain poor brother had but a single sleeping mat. He covered himself at night with one half of it, and lay upon the other half. Once, on a very cold night, the abbot of the monastery, walking by, overheard him saying: "I give Thee thanks O Lord! Here I am, like a king, stretching out my legs and moving as freely as I please, while there are so many people, many wealthy men, in prison; men sitting in irons, shackled with steel, or with their feet in the stocks!"

This is the first point: the example of poverty.

10. The second reason that should inflame you with love for poverty is the divine promise, beyond price. O good Lord Jesus, *rich towards all!* Who could worthily express in words, feel in his heart, or describe with his pen the heavenly glory You have promised to Your poor? By their free choice of poverty, they deserve "to stand in the presence of the Creator," to *enter into the powers of the Lord*, into that eternal tabernacle, into those mansions ablaze with lights; they deserve to be the citizens of that city established and built by God. For You have promised in Your own holy words: "*Blessed are the poor in spirit, for theirs is the kingdom of heaven.*"

O Lord Jesus Christ, the kingdom of heaven is nothing but Yourself, *the King of kings and Lord of lords*. It is Yourself whom You give to the poor as a prize, a reward, and a joy. It is You they will taste, You they will enjoy, with You they will be filled. *The lowly shall eat their fill; they who seek the Lord shall praise Him:* "*May your hearts be ever merry!*"

Chapter IV—On Silence and Quiet

1. The virtue of silence is of great help to the religious striving for perfection; for as, *where words are many, sin is not wanting*, so where words are few and short, sin is kept away. Much talk often results in offending both God and neighbor, while silence nourishes the tree of justice, from which is gathered the fruit of peace. And peace being essential to those who live in a cloister, so also is silence, preserving peace of heart and body. The prophet Isaias, considering the virtue of silence, has this to say: *The work of justice shall be peace; and the service of justice silence*; meaning that such is the power of silence that it preserves God's justice in man, and fosters and guards peace among neighbors. A man who fails to keep careful watch over his words will soon have wasted the gifts of grace he has received: he will soon be rushing headlong into many evils. As James says in his Epistle, *the tongue also is a little member, but it boasts mightily.... And the tongue is a fire, the very world of iniquity*. And the gloss explains here that "it is by means of the tongue that almost every misdeed is either planned or committed."

Handmaid of God, do you wish to hear, do you wish to know, how great are the evils of a tongue imperfectly controlled? Listen, and I will tell you. From the tongue are born blasphemies, complaints, excuses for sin, perjury, lies, detraction, flattery, cursing, wrangling, arguing, scoffing at virtue, bad advice, gossiping, boastful talk, the revelation of secrets, wild threats or promises, loquacity, and scurrility. Indeed, it would be a cause of shame for women in general, but it is most unworthy of consecrated virgins, not to control their words, and not to discipline their speech; for many misdeeds are committed by means of a reckless tongue. And I affirm it as a certainty that it is useless for a religious to pride herself on the virtue in her heart as long as the discipline of silence is laid waste by the disturbance of loquacity. The Scriptures say: *If anyone thinks himself to be religious, not restraining his tongue but deceiving his own heart, that man's religion is vain.*

2. Beloved brides of Jesus Christ, look upon your Lady and mine; behold Mary, the mirror of all virtues, and learn from her the discipline of silence. It is easy to see from the Gospels how quiet the Blessed Virgin was, speaking very little, and with few people; it is recorded that she talked to four, and spoke seven times: twice to the angel, twice to Elizabeth, twice to her Son, and once to the attendants at the wedding. Thus is our loquacity put to shame, in that we tend to talk too much, forgetting that silence is of such great worth.

3. One of the advantages of silence is the sorrow it induces in our hearts. While a man is holding his tongue, he considers his ways and can realize how abundant are his defects, how slight his progress, and from this comes a repentant heart. The prophet David says: "*I kept dumb and silent; I refrained from rash speech. But my grief was stirred up.*"[40]

Another advantage of silence is that it shows man to be heavenly. An almost incontrovertible argument would be this: Suppose a man lives in Germany and speaks no German: it would appear that he is not a German. Similarly, if a man lives in the world and speaks not the language of the world: this shows clearly that he is not of the world. *He who is from the earth ... of the earth he speaks*, as is said in the Gospel of John.

Nothing better helps a religious to remain silent than flight from the company of others and the pursuit of a life of solitude. The man who has already risen above the contingencies of human existence has need of no other consoler or interlocutor than God. Hence, he should live in peace and solitude. Having God as a companion, he is not to be concerned with the company of men. Thus, it is said in the third book of Lamentations: *He shall sit solitary and hold his peace: because he hath taken it up upon himself.*[41] He shall sit solitary by avoiding the company of men, he shall hold his peace by meditating upon the joys of

---

[40] This is another example of literal quotation of the Scriptures outside of context: grief was not stirred up by the effort of remaining silent, but by the presence of a wicked man.

[41] This is the Challoner-Douay translation of the Vulgate text, "levavit super se." Bonaventure has "levavit se supra se."

heaven, and he has risen above his state by tasting celestial delights.

4. Although silence is a necessity for any religious who seeks perfect virtue, the preserving of its discipline is most essential to the virgins dedicated to God, the handmaids of Jesus Christ. They should be reserved in their words in the measure in which they consider speech to be precious, so that they speak only when they must. Blessed Jerome says: "May the words of a virgin be humble and few, and may their value come rather from modesty than from eloquence." A philosopher also gives the same advice: "For the sake of the highest perfection, I desire you to speak shortly, seldom, and in a low voice."

Listen, you talkative servant; you clamoring and garrulous virgin, attend! To become accustomed to silence, you should follow the example of Abbot Agathon, of whom we read in the "Lives of the Fathers" that he kept a pebble in his mouth for three years, until he had learned to be silent. You too should tie a pebble to your tongue, fix it to your palate, and *put your hand over your mouth*, so as to learn how to be silent. For it is most unbecoming that the brides of Christ should wish to converse with any other than their Spouse.

5. Speak seldom, with economy and brevity; speak with reverence and modesty; and, in your own cause scarcely speak at all. Cover your face with the veil of decency, sew your lips shut with the thread of discipline, let your words be brief, rare, to the point, as well as meek and humble. Handmaid of God, speak seldom and sparely, for *where words are many, sin is not wanting*. Never fall into idle speech, for *of every idle word men speak, they shall give account on the day of judgment*. As the gloss explains, "a word is idle when said without need, and heard without gain." It is, therefore, always better to remain silent than to speak, for, as a wise man says, "I have sometimes regretted having spoken, but never, having held my tongue."

Chapter V—On Assiduity in Prayer

1. It is very important for the bride of Christ who wishes to advance in perfection to train her soul in constant prayer and devotional exercises. For, truly, a lukewarm and indifferent religious who fails to pray constantly is not only a wretched and useless creature; she is, in fact, bearing before God a dead soul in a living body. The power of devotion is so great that it prevails over the temptations and snares of the vicious enemy—the only one who can prevent the handmaid of God from rising toward heaven. We cannot wonder, then, that the religious who fails to pray with constancy is often and miserably overcome by the tempter. Hence blessed Isidore says: "This is the remedy for one who burns with vicious temptations: every time the flame of any vice touches him, let him pray, for frequent prayer puts out such fires." The Lord also says in the Gospel: "*Watch and pray, that you may not enter into temptation.*"

Such is the power of devout prayer that it applies to all circumstances, and we profit by it at all times: in winter and summer, in sunshine and rain, by night and by day, on feast days and work days, in illness and health, in youth and old age, while standing, sitting, or walking, in choir or out of choir. Further than this: sometimes, by a single hour spent in prayer, more is gained than the whole world, for even a small prayer devoutly recited may assure us the kingdom of heaven. And so, in order that you may know how to pray and what to say, I will give you as much as the Lord gives me, although in this matter my need for enlightenment is even greater than yours.

2. Know, therefore, worthy handmaid of God, that to achieve perfection in prayer you must do three things:

FIRST, as soon as you have set yourself to pray, straightening your body and lifting up your heart, with all your senses closed, EXAMINE EVERY ONE OF YOUR FAILINGS with a sorrowful and contrite heart, considering the past, the present, and the future.

Begin by carefully recalling all the great sins you have committed throughout your life: all the great chances for good you have wasted both in the world and in the Order, all the great favors you have received from your Creator and so often lost. Consider also how far you have strayed from God because of sin, while you had been once so close to Him; how different you have become from God, while you had been once His very likeness; how beautiful in former days had been your soul, now so ugly and vile! Think of where sin is leading you: to the gates of hell. Think of what is coming upon you: the frightful day of judgment. Think of what you will be given for all this: the blasting flame of eternal death.

Therefore, strike your breast without delay, like the publican; like the prophet David, *roar with anguish of heart;* and, with Mary Magdalene, bathe the feet of the Lord Jesus with your tears. Weep without restraint, for you have offended your beloved Christ without restraint. This is precisely what blessed Isidore says: "When our prayer brings us in the presence of God, we should weep and lament, remembering how serious are the sins we have committed and how cruel the pains of the hell we dread." Such tearful meditation should begin your prayer.

3. The SECOND THING a bride of God must do when she prays is to GIVE THANKS. Let her in all humility thank the Creator for the favors already received and for those yet to come. The apostle Paul writes to the same purpose in the Epistle to the Colossians: *Be assiduous in prayer, being wakeful therein with thanksgiving.* Nothing makes one more deserving of God's gifts than to thank Him again and again for the graces He has granted so far. Blessed Augustine expresses the same to Aurelius in these terms: "What better could be thought, said, or written than 'Thank God'? There is no shorter saying, no happier sound, no richer meaning, no more fruitful act, than this."

While praying, remember with a grateful heart: God made you a human being; He made you a Christian; He forgave your countless sins; He watched over you so that you should not fall into many more iniquities; He did not let you perish in the world but chose for you the highest and most perfect type of religious life; He sustained you and is still sustaining you without any merit on your part; for your sake, He became man, was circumcised and baptized; He became poor and naked, humble and despised; He fasted and knew hunger and thirst, toil and weariness; He wept, He sweated blood, He gave you His most sacred body for food and His most precious blood for drink; He was struck in the face, spat upon, mocked, scourged; He was crucified, wounded, and made to die the most cruel and disgraceful death. That was the price He paid for you. Remember: He was buried, then rose from the dead and ascended into heaven; He sent down the Holy Spirit; and He promised the kingdom of heaven to you and to all His chosen ones.

Such gratitude is immensely helpful when you pray, since without it, no prayer has any value. Blessed Bernard says: "Ingratitude is a burning wind that dries up the fountain of piety, the dew of mercy, and the flow of grace."

4. The THIRD CONDITION of perfect prayer is that YOUR MIND BE CONCERNED WITH NOTHING BUT WHAT YOU ARE PRAYING FOR. It is most unbecoming that a man pray to God with his lips but apply his mind to some other thought, so that one half of his heart is lifted up to heaven, while the other is chained to earth. God never heeds such a prayer. The gloss on the passage of the Psalm, *I call out with all my heart; answer me,* O *Lord,* explains that "a divided heart obtains nothing."

At the time of prayer, the handmaid of the Lord should turn her heart away from all external care, worldly desire, and casual affection, and concentrate on interior things, tending with her whole heart and mind toward Him alone who is the object of her invocation. As your Spouse Jesus Christ advises in the Gospel: "*When thou prayest, go into thy room, and closing thy door, pray to thy Father.*" You go into your room when you collect all your thoughts, desires, and affections in the secret of your heart; you close your door when you so carefully guard your heart that no fanciful flight of imagination can disturb your devotion.

Augustine says that "prayer is the turning of the mind toward God through the pious and humble movement of the heart."

5. Listen, dearest Mother, handmaid of Jesus Christ, *incline your ears to the words of my mouth.* Make no mistake, be not deceived; waste not the rich fruit of your prayer; lose not its suavity; be not robbed of the sweetness you should draw from it. Prayer is a vessel with which the grace of the Holy Spirit is drawn from that overflowing font of delight, the most blessed Trinity. The holy prophet David knew it well when he said: *I opened my mouth, and panted.* The gloss supplies an interpretation of these words of the prophet: " 'I opened my mouth' stands for praying, seeking, requesting; and 'panted' means 'I inhaled the Spirit.' "

Have I not already told you what, prayer is? Listen again: prayer consists in turning the mind toward God. Do you wish to know how to turn your mind toward God? Follow my words. When you pray, gather up your whole self, enter with your Beloved into the chamber of your heart, and there remain alone with Him, forgetting all exterior concerns; and so rise aloft with all your love and all your mind, your affection, desire, and devotion. And let not your mind wander away from your prayer, but rise again and again in the fervor of your piety until you enter *into the place of the wonderful tabernacle, even to the house of God.* There, your heart will be delighted at the sight of your Beloved, and you will *taste and see how good the Lord is*, and how great is His goodness. You will rush into His embrace, will kiss Him with such intimate fervor that you will be completely carried away, wholly enraptured in heaven, fully transformed into Christ. Unable to contain yourself, you will cry out with the prophet David: *My soul refused to be comforted: I remembered God, and was delighted.*

6. Beloved Mother, if devout prayer is to raise your heart even higher and make it burn with still more ardent love for God, consider carefully that three things may lift the soul in ecstasy: the height of devotion, of admiration, or of exultation.

7. First, the height of DEVOTION sometimes may cause our spirit "to lose hold of itself and rise above itself"; to pass into a state of rapture "when we are inflamed with the ardor of such celestial desire that the whole world seems bitter and tiresome. This flame of intimate love, grown beyond human measure, makes the soul to swoon, to melt like wax, and to rise aloft like incense, higher and higher, to the very summit." Then we cannot help but cry out with the prophet: *Though my flesh and my heart waste away, God is the rock of my heart and my portion forever.*

8. Again, rapture sometimes occurs because of the height of ADMIRATION. "When our soul is irradiated with divine light, and held in suspense by the wonder of the supreme Beauty, it is thrown off its foundation. In the likeness of a flash of lightning, the deeper the soul is cast into the abyss by the contrast between the unseen Beauty and itself, the higher and the faster does it rise to the sublime, borne as it is above itself by the ardor of its lofty desires." Then our soul is driven to exclaim with blessed Esther: *I saw Thee, my Lord, as an angel of God: and my heart was troubled for fear of Thy majesty. For Thou, my Lord, art very admirable: and Thy face is full of graces.*

9. Finally, rapture may come about through the height of EXULTATION. Once our soul has tasted this intimate abundance of internal sweetness, or rather, when it is fully inebriated, it completely forgets what it is and what it was, and its whole being becomes supernatural desire, carried away as it is in a state of wonderful happiness." Then, irresistibly, it raises the prophet's chant: *How lovely is Your dwelling place, O Lord of Hosts! My soul yearns and pines for the*

courts of the Lord. My heart and my flesh cry out for the living God.

10. Thus should the handmaid of God train herself to become assiduous in prayer, and learn through its unwearied use, through the vision of a cleansed and purified heart, through a spirit of devotion ever renewed, to essay contemplation of the divine mysteries and enjoyment of the sweetness of divine delights. It is not fitting that the soul, stamped with God's image, adorned with His likeness, redeemed by His blood, and called to beatific vision, should flutter around worldly vanities. Rather, it should mount a Cherub and fly, borne on the wings of the wind; that is, ascend with the choirs of angels to contemplate the Trinity Itself and the humanity of Christ, and to meditate on the glory and joy of the citizens of heaven, the angels and saints.

But how many today would apply themselves to such meditations, explore the celestial joys, and dwell in heaven with heart and mind? Very few indeed. We may fittingly apply to some religious what blessed Bernard says: "Those very men who should be busy storming heaven with their devotion, mentally visiting the celestial mansions, greeting the apostles, and admiring the triumphant choirs of prophets and martyrs, lay all this aside and surrender to the debasing servitude of the body in order to obey their lust and satisfy their gluttony."

Chapter VI—On Remembering the Passion of Christ

1. Since fervor of devotion is nourished and preserved in us by a frequent return of our thoughts to the passion of Christ, anyone who wishes to keep the flame of ardor alive within himself should frequently—or rather, incessantly—contemplate in his heart Christ dying upon the cross. That is why the Lord said of old: *The fire on the altar is to be kept burning; it must not go out. Every morning the priest shall put firewood on it.*

Listen, devout Mother: your heart is the altar of God. It is here that the fire of intense love must burn always. You are to feed it every day with the wood of the cross of Christ and the commemoration of His passion. The prophet Isaias says: *You shall draw waters with joy out of the Saviour's fountains;* meaning that whoever wishes to obtain from God the waters of grace, the waters of devotion, the waters of tears, must draw from *the fountains* which are the five wounds of Christ.

2. Therefore, let your love lead your steps to Jesus wounded, to Jesus crowned with thorns, to Jesus fastened upon the gibbet of the cross. Not only *see in His hands the print of the nails*, with the apostle Thomas, not only put your finger into the place of the nails, not only put your hand into His side, but enter with your whole being through the door of His side into Jesus' heart itself. There, transformed into Christ by your burning love for the Crucified, pierced by the nails of the fear of God, wounded by the spear of superabounding love, transfixed by the sword of intimate compassion, seek nothing, desire nothing, wish for no consolation, other than to be able to die with Christ on the cross. Then you may cry out with the apostle Paul: *With Christ, I am nailed to the cross. It is now no longer I that live, but Christ lives in me.*

3. Now, this is the way you should keep in mind the passion of Christ. Consider how utterly degrading it was; how bitterly cruel; how all-inclusive; and how long-drawn-out.

Consider first, honorable handmaid of God, that the death of your Spouse Jesus Christ was UTTERLY DEGRADING. He was hung on a tree like a robber and a thief. Under the Old Law, such punishment was reserved for the worst and most atrocious criminals, and for robbers and thieves. Next, consider a greater insult to Christ: He was crucified on Mount Calvary, a most infamous and loathsome place, strewn with the bones and bodies of many dead; for this was the spot where the death sentences were carried out; here the vilest of men were beheaded and their bodies strung up. Again, consider a still greater insult to Christ: He was hanged as a thief among thieves, and in the central place as a prince of thieves. This is why Isaias says that He *was reputed with the wicked*. Finally, consider the greatest insult of all to be inflicted upon your Spouse: He was left in mid-air, suspended between heaven and earth. Oh, the worth of such unworthiness and shame! The whole earth is denied to the Sovereign of the earth; nothing in the world is deemed less noble than the Lord of the world Himself. Thus, the death of the Son of God was utterly degrading because of the kind of death—He was suspended on the cross; because of the companions of death—He was reckoned and condemned among the wicked; because of the place of death—He was crucified in the stench of Mount Calvary.

4. O good Jesus, kind Saviour, it was not once but many times that You were affronted; for when a man is insulted in many ways, he becomes so much the more contemptible to the world. O Lord Jesus, they bind You in the Garden, they strike Your face in the house of Annas, they spit upon You in the courtyard of Caiphas, they mock You in the palace of Herod; they make You carry the cross along the road, and crucify You on Golgotha. Alas, alas! The Liberator of Captives is caught; the Glory of the Angels is derided; the Life of Men is put to death! O wretched Jews, how well you have fulfilled your intent!—for you had said: "*Let us condemn Him to a shameful death.*"

Blessed Bernard says: "*He emptied Himself, taking the nature of a slave.* He was the Son, and He became the slave. He assumed not only the slave's nature, in that He was subject to men, but also the evils of slavery, for He was flogged and forced to pay for a crime without being guilty." He was not only the Servant of the servants of God, as the Pope is; He even became the Servant of the servants of Satan, serving to wash away the smallest sins of sinners. And still He was not satisfied, for He chose the most degrading of all deaths to hearten you for similar suffering. *He humbled Himself, becoming obedient to death, even to death on a cross;* "since this is more debasing," as the gloss explains.

5. Secondly, consider with attention, virgin consecrated to God, that the passion of Christ was BITTERLY CRUEL. The blessed limbs, stretched as they were upon the cross, could not be bent to give any measure of the relief instinctively sought in this way by a man in agony; nor was there any support for His sacred head when He was about to give up His soul.

You will see even more clearly how cruel was the death of Christ if you consider that whatever is more sensitive suffers more. In general, the body of a woman is more sensitive than that of a man; but never was there a body that felt pain as keenly as that of the Saviour, since His flesh was entirely virginal: conceived of the Holy Spirit and born of the Virgin. Hence the passion of Christ was as much more painful as He Himself was more tender even than any virgin. If His spirit, because of the tenderness of His flesh, was saddened by the mere thought of death, to the point where *His sweat became as drops of blood running down upon the ground*, how much more must He have suffered, how intense must have been His pain, in the cruel passion itself!

Blessed Bernard says: "The torments of Your heart, O Lord Jesus, were clearly revealed by the sweat of blood that ran from Your blessed flesh down upon the ground at the time of Your prayer." And Anselm: "What have You done, O Beloved, to be treated in this fashion? What crime have You committed, O Most Loving, to be condemned as You are? Behold, I am the cause of Your suffering, I am the wound of which You have died."

And now, consider with even greater attention how bitter was the death of Christ. The more innocent a man is, the heavier he will find the burden of punishment. If it had been for His own sins that Christ suffered these pains, He would have borne them somewhat more easily. But He was the One *who did not sin, neither was deceit found in His mouth.* Pilate is a witness to this, as his words show: "*I find no guilt in Him.*" For Christ is *the refulgence of eternal light, the spotless mirror of the power of God, the image of His goodness*, as is said in the Book of Wisdom.

6. Consider more fully yet how filled with torment was the death of your beloved Spouse. The more INCLUSIVE a pain is, the harder it is to bear. Christ, your Spouse, suffered in every part of His body. No portion was small enough to be spared its own pain, no area too minute to be void of bitter suffering. *From the sole of the foot unto the top of the head, there is no soundness therein.* Wherefore, in the excess of His torment, He cried out: "O *all ye that*

pass by the way, attend, and see if there be any sorrow like to My sorrow!

Indeed, no sorrow was ever comparable to Yours, O Lord Jesus Christ! Your blood was shed so abundantly that Your whole body was soaked with it. Not just a drop, O good Jesus, most sweet Lord! but a welling stream of blood sprang from five parts of Your body: the hands and feet in the crucifixion, the head in the crowning of thorns, the whole body in the flagellation, and the heart in the opening of Your side. Not an ounce of blood could have possibly remained in Your veins. Tell me, I beg You, most beloved Lord: why did You let Your blood pour forth in a river when a single drop would have sufficed for the redemption of the world? I know, Lord, I know in all truth that You did this for no other reason than to show the depth of Your love for me!

7. *How shall I make a return to the Lord for all the good He has done for me?* "Most surely, O Lord, as long as I live, I will remember the fatigue of Your constant preaching, the weariness of Your many travels, the prayerful watches, the tears of compassion, the sorrow, the abuse, the spittle, the blows, the mockeries, the nails, and the wounds; otherwise at my hand there will be required *all the just blood that has been shed on the earth."—Who will give water to my head and a fountain of tears to my eyes, and I will weep day and night* over the death of my Lord Jesus, which He suffered not for His sins but for mine. *He was wounded for our iniquities: He was bruised for our sins*, as the prophet Isaias exclaims.

8. Finally, consider with the very greatest attention HOW LONG-DRAWN-OUT were Christ's sufferings before He died. From the first day of His life to the last, from the instant of birth to the instant of death, pain and sorrow were His companions. So He Himself has said through the prophet: "*I am afflicted and in agony from My youth*"; and elsewhere: "*I have been scourged all the day*," meaning all His life.

And now, from a different viewpoint, consider how the suffering of Christ was extended. They crucified Him in order to lengthen His passion, to protract His pain and exclude an early end to His agony, to postpone His death and thus torture Him longer and abuse Him more severely.

9. From all such hardships, as I have explained, you may conclude, O virgin of Christ and handmaid of God, how degrading, cruel, inclusive, and lengthy was the passion and death of your most beloved Spouse Jesus Christ. He withstood all these sufferings in order to set you aflame with love for Him; in order to move you, in return, to love Him with all your heart, all your soul, and all your mind. What could be more generous than that God should take the nature of a slave for the slave's redemption? What better lesson leads man to salvation than the example of a death suffered for the sake of divine justice and obedience? What better reason for man to love God than the tremendous loving-kindness of the Son of God in laying down His life for us—with, on our part, no merit, but rather many sins? This implies goodness in so exalted a degree that nothing more merciful, more generous, or more kind can be imagined. Such goodness appears the greater, the heavier and more shameful the burden which Christ not only sustained, but actually chose to bear for us. For *He who has not spared even His own Son but has delivered Him for us all, how can He fail to grant us also all things with Him?* Thus, we are invited to love Him, and in loving Him, to follow His example.

10. Woe to those who show no gratitude for the graces purchased by such great goodness, and upon whose souls the death of Christ has no effect. "Behold," says Bernard, "the head of Christ leaning down to kiss us, His arms stretched out for an embrace, His hands pierced for a gift of blood, His side opened for loving, His whole body extended for a complete spending of Himself." Woe to those who *crucify again for themselves the Son of God*, adding to the pain of Him they have wounded. Woe also to those whose hearts not even such bloodshed, not even the payment of such a price, can soften with pity, inspire with kindness, inflame with zeal for good. Assuredly, these *enemies of the cross of Christ* are hurling at the Son of God—now enthroned in heaven at the right hand of the Father—worse blasphemies than did the Jews of old while He hung on the cross. These are the kind of men to whom and of whom the Lord complains through blessed Bernard, when He says: "Behold, O man, what I suffer for you: can any pain be compared to the pain of My cross? I cry to you, I who die for you: behold the punishment I have to bear, behold the nails that pierce My flesh. Yet, cruel as the exterior pain may be, My inner pain is worse when I am faced with your ingratitude."

11. Beware, Mother, beware lest you too forget such favors; lest you too be ungrateful for the immeasurable price which was paid for you. Place Jesus Christ crucified *as a seal on your heart;* like a seal pressed down upon softened wax, imprint your Spouse thereon, saying with the prophet: "*My heart has become like wax melting away.*" Place Him also *as a seal on your arm*, so as never to cease doing good, never to weary of laboring in the name of the Lord Jesus; and when all is done, to begin again as if you had done nothing.

If, at times, things sad, burdensome, tiring, or bitter happen along your way, particularly if some good appears distasteful, run without delay to Jesus on the cross. Look at His crown of thorns, His iron nails, and the spear in His side; contemplate the wounds of the hands and feet, the wounds of the head and side, the wounds of the whole body; remember who it was that suffered so bitterly and bore such outrage for you, and how He must have loved you. Believe me, at the thought you will instantly find every sadness joyful, every burden light, every chore a pleasure, and every hardship sweet, so that you also will cry out, like blessed Job: "*The things which before my soul would not touch*, now, through the anguish of the passion of Christ, have become my food"; as if you were saying: "Those goods which at first my soul did not savor, now, because of the torments of Christ's suffering, which I behold, have become sweet and delightful to me."

Thus, we read that a certain man who had embraced the religious life was much tried by the severity of the rules concerning food, and the general discipline of the cloister. When his patience was at an end, he fell on his knees before an image of the Crucified and began tearfully to complain of the intolerable hardship and strain he was suffering in the Order, and of the tastelessness of the food and drink. Immediately there commenced to flow from the side of the image a stream of blood; and while this man so freely lamented and bewailed his troubles, the image of Christ answered him, saying that each time he found the food and drink unpalatable, he was to mix them with the condiment of Christ's blood.

Chapter VII—On Perfect Love for God

1. Handmaid of God, I have taught you as God moved me to do, how to train your soul for a gradual ascent, and how to *go from strength to strength*. Now, in this seventh chapter, we have to deal with the very essence of all virtue, that is, love, which alone leads man to perfection. As a means of uprooting vice, advancing in grace, and achieving the highest proficiency in holiness, there is no better word, no better thought, than love. Prosper says in his book "On Contemplative Life": "Love is the life of virtue and the death of vice." *As wax melts before the fire*, so vice perishes before love. Such is the power of love that it alone closes hell, opens heaven, restores the hope of salvation, and makes a soul agreeable to God. Such is the power of love that, of all the virtues, it is

called "the virtue," for with it a man is rich, fortunate, and happy, and without it he is a naked and miserable beggar.

Explaining these words of the Epistle to the Corinthians, *If I ... do not have charity*, the gloss says: "See how great charity is, for in its absence all virtues are worthless, while in its presence all virtues are implied. As soon as a man begins to love, he possesses the Holy Spirit." And blessed Augustine: "If virtue is that which leads us to eternal life, I would say that virtue is nothing but the highest love for God." Now, since charity is so exalted, we should strive for it more than for any other virtue. Note that charity should not be just any love, but such love as loves God above all else, and the neighbor for the sake of God.

2. Your Spouse Himself, speaking in the Gospel, teaches you how much you are to love your Creator: "*Thou shalt love the Lord thy God with thy whole heart, and with thy whole soul, and with thy whole mind.*" Beloved handmaid of Jesus Christ, examine carefully what kind of love your most sweet Jesus expects of you. Your great Lover certainly wants you to give Him your whole heart, soul, and mind, so that there may be absolutely no one else in heart, soul, and mind to share your love with Him.

What should you do to be certain that you love the Lord God with your whole heart? What is this "whole heart"? Listen to blessed John Chrysostom teaching you: "To love God with your whole heart means that your heart should not tend to love any other thing more than God; that you should not find a greater delight in the world, in honors, or in family ties than you do in God. If the love of your heart is engaged in any of these things, you do not love God with your whole heart."

I beg you, servant of Christ, make no mistake in this matter of love. If you love something, and this love is not in God or for the sake of God, you can be sure that you do not love God with your whole heart. Therefore Augustine says: "O Lord, he loves You less who loves something besides You." Thus, if you love something, but this affection fails to increase your love for God, you do not love with your whole heart. And if you love something, but because of this love you forget what you owe Christ, you do not love with your whole heart. Hence, love the Lord your God with your whole heart.

3. You should love your Lord Jesus Christ not only with your whole heart, but also with your whole soul. What is your "whole soul"? Listen to blessed Augustine teaching you: "To love God with your whole soul means to love Him with your whole will, excluding any interference." You can be sure of loving with your whole soul when, willingly and without reluctance, you accomplish what you know to be the will of your Lord, instead of following your own will, the world's advice, or the promptings of the flesh. Certainly you love God with your whole soul when you are ready to die for the love of Jesus Christ, if called upon to do so. Should you be deficient in any of these points, you do not love with your whole soul. Hence, love the Lord your God with your whole soul by conforming your will to His in everything.

4. It is not only with your whole heart and your whole soul that you are to love your Spouse, the Lord Jesus, but also with your whole mind. What is your "whole mind"? Listen again to blessed Augustine teaching you: "To love God with your whole mind is to love Him with your whole memory, without forgetfulness."

Chapter VIII—On Final Perseverance

1. The ACQUISITION of the principle of all virtues is not enough to make one appear glorious in the eyes of the Lord; PERSEVERANCE, the crown of virtue, must also be there. No mortal, however perfect he may be, should be praised in his lifetime until he has completed well and successfully the good work he had started. Perseverance is the achievement and "the consummation of virtue, the mother of merit, and the means to the reward," as Bernard says. And he adds: "Take away perseverance, and neither will obedience or kindness give rise to grace, nor steadfastness earn praise." It is of little use for a man to have been religious, patient, humble, devout, and chaste, to have loved God and practiced all the other virtues, if he fails to persevere. Even though all the virtues run in

the race, perseverance alone *receives the prize*. The man who *will be saved* is not the one who starts, but the one *who has persevered to the end*. Wherefore, John Chrysostom says: "What good is a seedling that first grows, and then withers?" He means that it is no good at all.

2. Most beloved virgin of Christ, if you have any good habits, or rather because you have so many, profit by them; as a champion of Christ, practice them courageously until death, so that when you reach your last day and the end of your life, you may receive a crown of glory and honor as payment and reward for your effort. Jesus Christ, your only Beloved, speaks to you in the Apocalypse in these words: "*Be thou faithful unto death, and I will give thee the crown of life.*" This crown is, in truth, the reward of eternal life, which all Christians should ardently seek. It is indeed so great that, as Gregory says, "no man could measure its worth"; so varied that no man could count its joys; so long-lasting that it will never end.

This is the reward, this is the crown your beloved Spouse Jesus Christ offers you in the Canticle: "*Come from Libanus, My spouse, come from Libanus, come: thou shalt be crowned.*" Arise, beloved of God, spouse of Jesus Christ, dove of the eternal King, and come; hasten to the nuptial banquet of the Son of God, for all the heavenly court is expecting you, *and everything is ready*.

3. Awaiting you are an attendant fair and noble to serve you, food refined and delicious to sustain you, company most friendly and sweet to rejoice with you. Rise, therefore, and hurry to the wedding feast.

An attendant fair and noble waits to serve you: none other than the angelic choir—nay, the very Son of the eternal God Himself, as He promised in the Gospel when He said: "*Amen I say to you, He will gird Himself, and will make them recline at table, and will come and serve them.*" What glory unimaginable for the poor and the miserable to be served by the Son of God the supreme King, and by all the assembled hosts of the heavenly kingdom!

4. Delicious and refined food is ready for your sustenance. The Son of God will set the table with His own hands, as He promised in the Gospel: "*And I appoint to you a kingdom, even as My Father has appointed to Me, that you may eat and drink at My table in My kingdom.*" How ravishing to the taste is this food which in His goodness God has provided for the needy! Happy the man who, in the kingdom of heaven, shall eat of this bread, prepared by the fire of the Holy Spirit in the secret of the virginal womb! *If anyone eat of this bread he shall live forever.* This is the food and bread the heavenly King serves His elect at His table, as is said in the Book of Wisdom: *You nourished Your people with Food of angels, and furnished them bread from heaven, ready to hand, untoiled-for, endowed with all delights and conforming to every taste ... and serving the desire of him who received it.* Behold, such is the fare of the heavenly table.

5. A sweet and most friendly company is also there, ready to rejoice with you. For Jesus will be there, with the Father and the Holy Spirit; Mary, with the flowery throng of the virgins; the apostles, martyrs, and confessors, with the whole celestial army of the blest. How wretched the man who is excluded from this most elect company! How wholly dead the heart which does not even wish to join it!

6. As for you, chosen servant of Christ, I know that you desire Christ; I know that all your strength is directed toward this end—the discovery of the means by which you may meet the eternal King in a close union and embrace. So now, "prompt your heart and your soul; lift up your whole mind and consider as intently as you can:

"If good things are so pleasant even when enjoyed singly, imagine how delightful beyond delight that Good must be which contains the delightfulness of all goods! If life created is so precious, imagine how enrapturing must be Life All-creating! If salvation is our best end as an acquired state, how transporting must be Salvation Itself, the Author of all deliverance!... What will a man have who possesses that Good, and what will he not have? Assuredly, He will have everything that satisfies him, and nothing that displeases. *Eye has not seen nor ear heard, nor has it entered into the heart of man* what bodily and spiritual goods he will enjoy in heaven. Why, then, servant of God, do you wander so far, seeking delights for your body and mind? Love one single Good in which all goods are found, and that will suffice; desire a simple Good, which is all good, and that will be enough."

7. "That is where you will find what you love, what you desire, dear Mother, virgin of God. Tell me, what do you love, dear Mother? What do you desire, virgin of God? Anything you love, anything you desire, is here. If it is beauty you love, *the just will shine forth like the sun;* if it is a long and healthy life, here is eternal well-being, for *the just live forever,* and the salvation of the just is without end; if it is abundance, you will be satisfied when the glory of God appears; if it is inebriation, you will be inebriated with the plenty of God's house; if it is sweet music, here the choir of angels sings continuously the praise of God; if it is friendship, here the saints will love God more than themselves, and God will love them more than they love themselves. If it is peace you seek, they all will be of one mind, having no will but the will of God. If it is honor and riches, here God sets His good and faithful servants and handmaids over many things; and what is more, they shall be called His children. Wherever God shall be, there also shall they be found, for they are *heirs indeed of God and joint heirs with Christ."*

8. "How wonderful and great must be the joy whose object is so great and wonderful! Most certainly, O Lord Jesus, *eye has not seen nor ear heard, nor has it entered into the heart of man* in this present life what love belongs to Your elect in that blessed life." The more we love God here, the more we shall enjoy God there. Therefore, love God much in this life, and you shall enjoy Him much in the next; let the love of God increase in you now, so that you may have then the fullness of His joy." This is the truth to be pondered in your mind, proclaimed by your tongue, loved in your heart, expressed by your lips; your soul should hunger, your body thirst, your whole substance crave for nothing but this until you enter the joy of your God,"[42] until you are clasped in your Lover's arms, until you are led into the chamber of your beloved Spouse who, with the Father and the Holy Spirit, lives and reigns, one God, forever and ever. Amen.

---

[42] St. Bonaventure uses the same quotation from St. Anselm as a conclusion to the "Breviloquium," and the "Soliloquium."

ABOUT CROSSREACH PUBLICATIONS

Thank you for choosing CrossReach Publications.

Hope. Inspiration. Trust.

These three words sum up the philosophy of why CrossReach Publications exist. To create inspiration for the present thus inspiring hope for the future, through trusted authors from previous generations.

We are *non-denominational* and *non-sectarian*. We appreciate and respect what every part of the body brings to the table and believe everyone has the right to study and come to their own conclusions. We aim to help facilitate that end.

We aspire to excellence. If we have not met your standards please contact us and let us know. We want you to feel satisfied with your product. Something for everyone. We publish quality books both in presentation and content from a wide variety of authors who span various doctrinal positions and traditions, on a wide variety of Christian topics that will teach, encourage, challenge, inspire and equip.

We're a family-based home-business. A husband and wife team raising 8 kids. If you have any questions or comments about our publications email us at:

CrossReach@outlook.com

Don't forget you can follow us on Facebook and Twitter, (links are on the copyright page above) to keep up to date on our newest titles and deals.

BESTSELLING TITLES FROM CROSSREACH[43]

The Screwtape Letters
C. S. Lewis
$7.99
www.amazon.com/dp/1535260181

I have no intention of explaining how the correspondence which I now offer to the public fell into my hands.

There are two equal and opposite errors into which our race can fall about the devils. One is to disbelieve in their existence. The other is to believe, and to feel an excessive and unhealthy interest in them. They themselves are equally pleased by both errors and hail a

---

[43] Buy from CrossReach Publications for quality and price. We have a full selection of titles in print and eBook. All available on the Amazon and Createspace stores. You can see our full selection just by searching for CrossReach Publications in the search bar!

materialist or a magician with the same delight. The sort of script which is used in this book can be very easily obtained by anyone who has once learned the knack; but ill-disposed or excitable people who might make a bad use of it shall not learn it from me.

Readers are advised to remember that the devil is a liar. Not everything that Screwtape says should be assumed to be true even from his own angle. I have made no attempt to identify any of the human beings mentioned in the letters; but I think it very unlikely that the portraits, say, of Fr. Spike or the patient's mother, are wholly just. There is wishful thinking in Hell as well as on Earth.

A Grief Observed
C. S. Lewis
$6.99
www.amazon.com/dp/1534898409

No one ever told me that grief felt so like fear. I am not afraid, but the sensation is like being afraid. The same fluttering in the stomach, the same restlessness, the yawning. I keep on swallowing. At other times it feels like being mildly drunk, or concussed. There is a sort of invisible blanket between the world and me. I find it hard to take in what anyone says. Or perhaps, hard to want to take it in. It is so uninteresting. Yet I want the others to be about me. I dread the moments when the house is empty. If only they would talk to one another and not to me.

How to Be Filled with the Holy Spirit
A. W. Tozer
$9.99
www.amazon.com/dp/1517462282

Before we deal with the question of how to be filled with the Holy Spirit, there are some matters which first have to be settled. As believers you have to get them out of the way, and right here is where the difficulty arises. I have been afraid that my listeners might have gotten the idea somewhere that I had a how-to-be-filled-with-the-Spirit-in-five-easy-lessons doctrine, which I could give you. If you can have any such vague ideas as that, I can only stand before you and say, "I am sorry"; because it isn't true; I can't give you such a course. There are some things, I say, that you have to get out of the way, settled.

The Two Babylons
Alexander Hislop
$8.99
www.amazon.com/dp/1523282959

Fully Illustrated High Res. Images. Complete and Unabridged.
Expanded Seventh Edition. This is the first and only seventh edition available in a modern digital edition. Nothing is left out! New material not found in the first six editions!!! Available in eBook and paperback edition exclusively from CrossReach Publications.

"In his work on "The Two Babylons" Dr. Hislop has proven conclusively that all the idolatrous systems of the nations had their origin in what was founded by that mighty Rebel, the beginning of whose kingdom was Babel (Gen. 10:10)."—A. W. Pink, The Antichrist (1923)

There is this great difference between the works of men and the works of God, that the same minute and searching investigation, which displays the defects and imperfections of the one, brings out also the beauties of the other. If the most finely polished needle on which the art of man has been expended be subjected to a microscope, many inequalities, much roughness and clumsiness, will be seen. But if the microscope be brought to bear on the flowers of the field, no such result appears. Instead of their beauty diminishing, new beauties and still more delicate, that have escaped the naked eye, are forthwith discovered; beauties that make us appreciate, in a way which otherwise we could have had little conception of, the full force of the Lord's saying, "Consider the lilies of the field, how they grow; they toil not, neither do they spin: and yet I say unto you, That even Solomon, in all his glory, was not arrayed like one of these." The same law appears also in comparing the Word of God and the most finished productions of men. There are spots and blemishes in the most admired productions of human genius. But the more the Scriptures are searched, the more minutely they are studied, the more their perfection appears; new beauties are brought into light every day; and the discoveries of science, the researches of the learned, and the labours of infidels, all alike conspire to illustrate the wonderful harmony of all the parts, and the Divine beauty that clothes the whole. If this be the case with Scripture in general, it is especially the case with prophetic Scripture. As every spoke in the wheel of Providence revolves, the prophetic symbols start into still more bold and beautiful relief. This is very strikingly the case with the prophetic language that forms the groundwork and corner-stone of the present work. There never has been any difficulty in the mind of any enlightened Protestant in identifying the woman "sitting on seven mountains," and having on her forehead the name written, "Mystery, Babylon the Great," with the Roman apostacy.

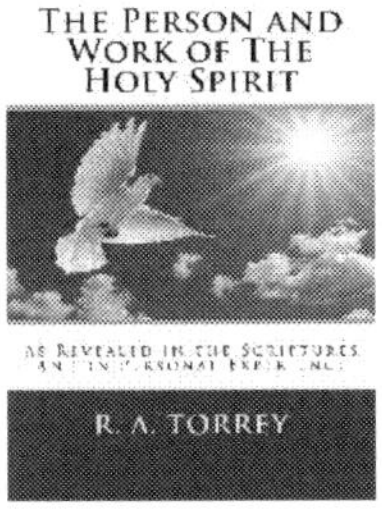

The Person and Work of the Holy Spirit
R. A. Torey
$5.75
www.amazon.com/dp/1533030308

BEFORE one can correctly understand the work of the Holy Spirit, he must first of all know the Spirit Himself. A frequent source of error and fanaticism about the work of the Holy Spirit is the attempt to study and understand His work without first of all coming to know Him as a Person.

It is of the highest importance from the standpoint of worship that we decide whether the Holy Spirit is a Divine Person, worthy to receive our adoration, our faith, our love, and our entire surrender to Himself, or whether it is simply an influence emanating from God or a power or an illumination that God imparts to us. If the Holy Spirit is a person, and a Divine Person, and we do not know Him as such, then we are robbing a Divine Being of the worship and the faith and the love and the surrender to Himself which are His due.

The Problem of Pain
C. S. Lewis
$6.99
www.amazon.com/dp/1535052120

When Mr. Ashley Sampson suggested to me the writing of this book, I asked leave to be allowed to write it anonymously, since, if I were to say what I really thought about pain, I should be forced to make statements of such apparent fortitude that they would become ridiculous if anyone knew who made them. Anonymity was rejected as inconsistent with the series; but Mr. Sampson pointed out that I could write a preface explaining that I did not live up to my own principles! This exhilarating programme I am now carrying out. Let me confess at once, in the words of good Walter Hilton, that throughout this book "I feel myself so far from true feeling of that I speak, that I can naught else but cry mercy and desire after it as I may". Yet for that very reason there is one criticism which cannot be brought against me. No one can say "He jests at scars who never felt a wound", for I have never for one moment been in a state of mind to which even the imagination of serious pain was less than intolerable. If any man is safe from the danger of under-estimating this adversary, I am that man. I must add, too, that the only purpose of the book is to solve the intellectual problem raised by suffering; for the far higher task of teaching fortitude and patience I was never fool enough to suppose myself qualified, nor have I anything to offer my readers except my conviction that when pain is to be borne, a little courage helps more than much knowledge, a little human sympathy more than much courage, and the least tincture of the love of God more than all.

Out of the Silent Planet
C. S. Lewis
$7.92
www.amazon.com/dp/1536869929

The last drops of the thundershower had hardly ceased falling when the Pedestrian stuffed his map into his pocket, settled his pack more comfortably on his tired shoulders, and stepped out from the shelter of a large chestnut-tree into the middle of the road. A violent yellow sunset was pouring through a rift in the clouds to westward, but straight ahead over the hills the sky was the colour of dark slate. Every tree and blade of grass was dripping, and the road shone like a river. The Pedestrian wasted no time on the landscape but set out at once with the determined stride of a good walker who has lately realized that he will have to walk farther than he intended. That, indeed, was his situation. If he had chosen to look back, which he did not, he could have seen the spire of Much Nadderby, and, seeing it, might have uttered a malediction on the inhospitable little hotel which, though obviously empty, had refused him a bed. The place had changed hands since he last went for a walking-tour in these parts. The kindly old landlord on whom he had reckoned had been replaced by someone whom the barmaid referred to as 'the lady,' and the lady was apparently a British innkeeper of that orthodox school who regard guests as a nuisance. His only chance now was Sterk, on the far side of the hills, and a good six miles away. The map marked an inn at Sterk. The Pedestrian was too experienced to build any very sanguine hopes on this, but there seemed nothing else within range.

Claiming Our Rights
E. W. Kenyon
$7.99
www.amazon.com/dp/1522757481

There is no excuse for the spiritual weakness and poverty of the Family of God when the wealth of Grace and Love of our great Father with His power and wisdom are all at our disposal. We are not coming to the Father as a tramp coming to the door begging for food; we come as sons not only claiming our legal rights but claiming the natural rights of a child that is begotten in love. No one can hinder us or question our right of approach to our Father.

Satan has Legal Rights over the sinner that God cannot dispute or challenge. He can sell them as slaves; he owns them, body, soul and spirit. But the moment we are born again... receive Eternal Life, the nature of God,—his legal dominion ends.

Christ is the Legal Head of the New Creation, or Family of God, and all the Authority that was given Him, He has given us: (Matthew 28:18), "All authority in heaven," the seat of authority, and "on earth," the place of execution of authority. He is "head over all things," the highest authority in the Universe, for the benefit of the Church which is His body.

Home Geography for the Primary Grades
C. C. Long
$7.95
www.amazon.com/dp/1518780660

A popular homeschooling resource for many generations now. Geography may be divided into the geography of the home and the geography of the world at large. A knowledge of the home must be obtained by direct observation; of the rest of the world, through the imagination assisted by information. Ideas acquired by direct observation form a basis for imagining those things which are distant and unknown. The first work, then, in geographical instruction, is to study that small part of the earth's surface lying just at our doors. All around are illustrations of lake and river, upland and lowland, slope and valley. These forms must be actually observed by the pupil, mental pictures obtained, in order that he may be enabled to build up in his mind other mental pictures of similar unseen forms. The hill that he climbs each day may, by an appeal to his imagination, represent to him the lofty Andes or the Alps. From the meadow, or the bit of level land near the door, may be developed a notion of plain and prairie. The little stream that flows past the schoolhouse door, or even one formed by the sudden shower, may speak to him of the Mississippi, the Amazon, or the Rhine. Similarly, the idea of sea or ocean may be deduced from that of pond or lake. Thus, after the pupil has acquired elementary ideas by actual perception, the imagination can use them in constructing, on a larger scale, mental pictures of similar objects outside the bounds of his own experience and observation.

In His Steps
Charles M. Sheldon
$4.99
www.amazon.com/dp/1535086262

The sermon story, In His Steps, or "What Would Jesus Do?" was first written in the winter of 1896, and read by the author, a chapter at a time, to his Sunday evening congregation in the Central Congregational Church, Topeka, Kansas. It was then printed as a serial in The Advance (Chicago), and its reception by the readers of that paper was such that the publishers of The Advance made arrangements for its appearance in book form. It was their desire, in which the author heartily joined, that the story might reach as many readers as possible, hence succeeding editions of paper-covered volumes at a price within the reach of nearly all readers.

The story has been warmly and thoughtfully welcomed by Endeavor societies, temperance organizations, and Y. M. C. A.'s. It is the earnest prayer of the author that the book may go its way with a great blessing to the churches for the quickening of Christian discipleship, and the hastening of the Master's kingdom on earth.

Charles M. Sheldon.
Topeka, Kansas,
November, 1897.

WE OFFER A LARGE & GROWING SELECTION OF CHRISTIAN TITLES
ALL AVAILABLE ON THE AMAZON & CREATESPACE STORES
JUST SEARCH FOR CROSSREACH PUBLICATIONS!

PRICES SUBJECT TO CHANGE WITHOUT WARNING.

Printed in Poland
by Amazon Fulfillment
Poland Sp. z o.o., Wrocław